The Librarian's Guide to Homeschooling Resources

SUSAN G. SCHEPS

AMERICAN LIBRARY ASSOCIATION
Chicago and London
1998

While extensive effort has gone into ensuring the reliability of information ap-
pearing in this book, the publisher makes no warranty, express or implied, on
the accuracy or reliability of the information, and does not assume and hereby
disclaims any liability to any person for any loss or damage caused by errors
or omissions in this publication.

Project editor: Louise D. Howe

Cover design by Lesiak Design

Text design by Dianne M. Rooney

Composition by the dotted i in Sabon and Optima using QuarkXpress 3.32

Printed on 50-pound White Offset, a pH-neutral stock, and bound in 10-point
coated cover stock by McNaughton & Gunn

The paper used in this publication meets the minimum requirements of American National Standard for Information Sciences—Permanence of Paper for
Printed Library Materials, ANSI Z39.48-1992. ∞

Library of Congress Cataloging-in-Publication Data

Scheps, Susan G.
    The librarian's guide to homeschooling resources / Susan G. Scheps.
        p.   cm.
    Includes bibliographical references.
    ISBN 0-8389-0737-7
    1. Libraries—Services to families—United States.   2. Libraries and
    education—United States.   3. Home schooling—United States.
    I. Title.
    Z711.92.F34S34   1998
    021.2′4′0973—dc21   98-6218

Printed in the United States of America.

02 01 00 99   5 4 3 2

To Jo Ellen Sarff,
in appreciation

Contents

Preface

When *Homeschoolers and the Public Library,* the predecessor of this book, was published by the Public Library Association in 1993, it was estimated that between ten to twenty thousand and a million American children were being taught at home. Accurate statistics were unavailable because of the decentralized nature of the movement. Many homeschoolers did not belong to a national organization; local groups changed addresses and members frequently; many homeschoolers chose to remain anonymous due to lack of support from state and local school administrators; and a large percentage of the population did not approve of homeschoolers. Yet it was very apparent in the early 90s that more and more parents were choosing to home school their children, and libraries across the United States began to see more homeschoolers and to receive requests from them for special materials, services, and programs.

In fact, according to a study by Brian D. Ray, director of the National Home Education Research Institute, the number of home-schoolers has grown by at least 25 percent each year since 1990. In the fall of 1996, he estimated that there were 1.23 million children being taught at home.[1] Patricia Lines, senior research analyst with the U.S. Department of Education's Office of Educational Research and Improvement, estimated 500,000 homeschoolers in the United States and another 50,000 in Canada in 1996. That was 1 percent of the total school population and 10 percent of the privately schooled population. The Home School Legal Defense Association forecasts two

---

1. "Estimates of Home Schooling Families in the United States" from Cheryl Gorder, *Home Schools: An Alternative.* 4th ed. (Mesa, Ariz.: Blue Bird Publishing, 1996). Also available on Blue Bird Publishing Web site: http://www.bluebird1. com/news_images/figure1.html

million home schooled children by the year 2000 if the current growth rate continues.[2]

Homeschoolers have sometimes been viewed as religious fanatics, probably as a result of a lot of bad publicity by the media during the late 1960s and the 1970s. While a large percentage of homeschoolers do incorporate Christian or other religious values into their children's education, a growing number of families are homeschooling because their children have had negative school experiences or because they are dissatisfied in general with public school education, low academic standards, and crowded classrooms. Homeschooling the child who has learning problems, behavioral problems, or problems coping with the competitiveness and group-directed orientation of the traditional classroom can lead to positive educational and behavioral experiences that result from a relaxed and nurturing environment. Homeschooling allows a child the flexibility to learn on family trips or on spur-of-the-moment "field trips," to use the community as a classroom, to set goals for him- or herself, to volunteer for community service, to take on more responsibility in the household, to learn to balance a checkbook, plan an outing, plant a garden, or run a business. Schooling at home promotes family closeness and offers time for in-depth study of those subjects that the child finds interesting (i.e., self-motivated learning). Children who learn more rapidly can enrich their knowledge with additional courses or activities such as music or art lessons, nature studies, language classes, or advanced math or science courses at the university level. Education becomes a part of the child's life, rather than an experience that takes place in an isolated environment, and the parent becomes a facilitator of learning, rather than a provider of information. Finally, some families choose to homeschool because they live too far away to send their children to either the public school or a private school that supports their own philosophy.

Studies have shown that children who are schooled at home are doing as well as or better than children who are enrolled in public schools, and that they score as high as or higher than the national average on standardized achievement tests.

The homeschool experience allows for various kinds of socialization. Most families join with other families in local groups that share similar ideals in order to provide group experiences, such as plays, spelling bees, or the culmination of a unit of study (i.e., a historical period; a specific country or culture; a science day). During the past five years

---

2. Lines, Patricia M., "Home Schooling." *Eric Digest,* no. 95 (EDO-EA-95-3) April 1995.

or so, many statewide and regional organizations have been founded. In many states these larger organizations provide structure to the state's homeschoolers, offering such services to their members as legislative monitoring and lobbying on legal issues, networking of information, annual conferences, curriculum fairs and workshops, and other services and referrals that would otherwise be unavailable at the local level. Through lists of local, state, national, legal, and other special homeschooling organizations that are regularly published in *Home Education Magazine, Growing Without Schooling,* and other homeschooling periodicals, through E-mail and chatrooms, homeschooling families are able to network with each other as never before.

There are several other important reasons for the recent rapid growth in homeschooling. New curricula and correspondence programs are available—some via the Internet. The number of curriculum suppliers and the variety of materials they offer has burgeoned. A growing number of trade publishers offer special catalogs and direct sales to home educators. Homeschooling families have greater access to public school programs and, in some areas of the country, to school facilities, equipment, textbooks, and education specialists. Computers for the home have become more affordable, and the Internet offers educational and networking opportunities that were nonexistent even five years ago. Even more important is the fact that homeschooling is now legal in every state in the United States and in every Canadian province, and, although there are some states whose rules of compliance make homeschooling difficult, many state boards of education now include homeschooling regulations and guidelines on their Web sites, along with information about statewide and local homeschooling organizations. Some employ contact people who can help with specific problems, legal compliance, curriculum, and referral services. There has also been wider acceptance of home-schooled children by universities. Positive, informative articles about homeschoolers in nationally circulated newspapers *(The New York Times, The Wall Street Journal),* and popular periodicals *(Time, Newsweek, Money)* have upgraded public opinion.

This resource guide is designed to help librarians understand the needs of homeschoolers and serve them efficiently. It includes:

- Some basic problems that libraries have encountered in serving homeschoolers
- Some reasonable services that homeschoolers would like from libraries
- Information that will enable quick retrieval of state and provincial legal and curriculum compliance data

- Information on special materials and services offered by several libraries to homeschoolers in their communities, along with the name of a librarian who can be contacted for advice and support
- Listings of national, statewide, and regional homeschooling organizations with background information on each that includes philosophy, objectives, and services offered
- Listings of publishers and distributors of homeschooling curricula and materials and of correspondence schools that offer programs of study for homeschoolers
- A listing of magazines and newsletters published by and for homeschoolers
- A bibliography of articles on homeschooling from a variety of general periodicals and library publications
- An annotated bibliography of books and Web sites of interest to homeschoolers

PART I

Serving Homeschoolers

The relationship between public libraries and homeschoolers is an important one which, if properly nurtured, can prove beneficial to both parties. For the homeschooler, the library represents access to the world of information—a place where a child can learn to understand the ways in which knowledge is organized, an opportunity for community service, and, for some, a gathering place. Libraries offer access to expensive specialized online reference services, easy access to Web sites of other libraries, reference materials on CD-ROM, and online reserves that speed the conveyance of library materials from other areas of the state and the country. A 1997 study by Brian D. Ray (National Home Education Research Institute) showed that 53 percent of the homeschoolers surveyed visit a library at least once or twice each month; 47 percent reported that they go even more often. The whole group in the study averaged 3.8 monthly library visits.[1] Because homeschoolers are great fans of libraries, they can offer support on library levies and bond issues. Many home-schooled children welcome the opportunity to volunteer at the public library as a way of providing community service while enjoying the intergenerational experience that it offers.

---

1. Ray, Brian, *Strengths of Their Own—Home Schoolers Across America: Academic Achievement, Family Characteristics, and Longitudinal Traits* (Salem, Ore.: National Home Education Research Institute, 1997). Summary edition available on HSLDA Web site: http://www.hslda.org/media/statsandreports/ray1997/15.stm

Here are some things that you, the librarian, can do in order to better understand and serve your homeschooling clientele:

1. Read some articles or books on homeschooling or visit a Web site, such as Home Education Press, that offers a wide array of information.

2. Convince yourself and others on your staff that, whether or not you approve, homeschooling is a viable educational option, and the public library has an obligation to serve the needs of this segment of the population.

3. Consider offering special programming, such as an introduction to the library catalog or the Internet, if there is a growing number of homeschoolers in your community.

4. Attend a local or statewide homeschooling convention. If there is one in your region, set up an information table advertising your library's services. Talk to homeschoolers and publishers and familiarize yourself with some of the popular curriculum materials.

Potential Problems
in Serving Homeschoolers

Staff Bias against Homeschoolers

Library staff members must be taught to deal with negative feelings
they might have regarding homeschoolers and their children and to
treat them just as they do other patrons. Despite their personal atti-
tudes toward homeschoolers, staff will be better prepared to interact
with them if they are well informed on issues such as the philosophy
of homeschooling; its legal status—especially in your home state; and
some facts regarding achievement and socialization opportunities,
such as the information found in the preface to this book. If you are
aware of prejudicial feelings from the staff, you might consider a short
in-service workshop in which you provide them with the necessary information and have a frank group discussion in order to help stem any
negativity.

Censorship and Materials Purchasing

Those who home school for religious reasons sometimes challenge
materials in the collection that do not conform to their moral and eth-
ical standards. Public libraries need to discuss their selection policies
with the home school clientele, especially stressing the fact that the library must offer a broad range of materials for every kind of need and
various approaches to a subject. If there is a large number of homeschoolers in your area, you will want to consider purchasing some

value-based children's literature in order to accommodate their needs, as well as a small collection of textbooks. Ask the homeschooling parents what their needs are, and make your purchasing decisions accordingly.

All-encompassing Lessons

Homeschoolers tend to charge out all materials related to a topic (in various subject areas) at once. Because many home schools are interest-centered, even if a purchased curriculum is being used, the child often focuses on all aspects of a topic (using all sorts of materials) until his or her curiosity is satiated. Thus, when a family or a group of home-schoolers is concentrating on the same topic, depletion of the library collection becomes a serious problem. Homeschooling parents should be made aware of the importance of assignment alerts and of the librarian's need to put some materials on temporary reserve for use in the library. With your encouragement, they can learn to borrow a limited number of items at one time, rather than charging out materials for a whole unit of study at once. You might also consider offering an occasional workshop or booktalk in the library for homeschooling parents at which you acquaint them with materials on various topics or introduce them to new materials in the collection. Subject booklists are helpful, as well. If your library offers teachers' loans, you would be wise to extend the privilege to your homeschooling patrons.

Heavy Use of Interlibrary Loan

Extensive use of interlibrary loan can create additional expenses for both paperwork and postage. While libraries in urban areas often can obtain materials via local delivery from other nearby library systems or through regional associations, homeschoolers who use smaller libraries outside of urban areas may make heavy demands on the staff to obtain materials by mail from distant libraries. Limiting the number of books that can be requested at one time is one way to contain costs. Libraries located in areas where large numbers of requests are the norm might consider limiting the number of items that one person or family can obtain through interlibrary loan in any month or year and charging for postage on any items in excess of that number.

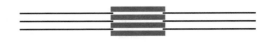

What Homeschoolers Want from Public Libraries

The following checklist draws on earlier lists provided by Janice Hedin, executive director of the Homeschoolers' Support Association (Washington), Susan Richman, editor of *Pennsylvania Homeschoolers,* and Susan Madden.

1. A file, regularly updated, that includes the following:
    a. The laws and compliance regulations of your state regarding homeschooling, as well as the name of the state superintendent (These can be obtained from your state Education Association)
    b. A directory of homeschooling support groups in the area
    c. Names and addresses of national and statewide homeschool organizations that can be contacted for information (see listings in this book)
    d. Addresses and names of contact people in local schools
    e. A listing of area agencies, museums, park services, associations that can be used as educational resources
    f. Booklists of library materials; lists of programs and services for children and groups
    g. A listing of suppliers of materials for homeschooling: publishers/distributors, correspondence schools, providers of learning and enrichment materials (or—even better—a collection of publishers' catalogs)
2. Workshops on how to use the library, including training on use of the Internet, the computer catalog, online reference services, and other reference sources

3. Library involvement with regional or state level homeschooling organizations (for example, by setting up a booth at the state or regional homeschool conference as a joint effort with one or more other libraries, making library brochures available, along with information on special services provided by the library)

4. A bulletin board in the library on which librarians and homeschoolers can display such things as:

    a. Statewide and local area meeting calendars, including library programs and other educational opportunities that are open to the public

    b. Information on contests (writing, poetry essay, art, music, etc.) for young people; science fairs; humanities programs; etc.

    c. Reviews of new books of interest to home-schooled children and their parents (on subjects such as keeping an organized home; reading aloud to children)

    d. Monthly pages from *Chase's Calendar of Events*

    e. Dates of book sales (library and others)

5. Regular displays of home school projects, art, hobbies, etc., in the library

6. Curriculum guides from local schools

7. Workshops on topics such as materials available in the library in various subject areas, new books, video recordings, CD-ROMs, and quality children's and parenting magazines

8. Tours of the library, along with information on obtaining interlibrary loans, accessing and making printouts of periodical articles, and use of in-house materials and services on CD-ROM

9. Special programs, e.g., a reading program during the school year for homeschoolers; special bibliographic instruction; programs offered by specialists in various subject areas (during the day)

10. A volunteer program. Home-schooled volunteers in libraries across the country have helped with fundraising projects such as book sales, lobbying for libraries, tutoring, reviewing books and audiovisual materials. They have also presented children's programs on topics they have studied and put on plays for children at the library. They are especially interested in intergenerational volunteer opportunities in which the children can have the opportunity to work alongside older community members.

11. Access to recent publishers' catalogs and book review journals

12. A good collection of audiotapes and compact discs

13. Use of the library's meeting room for group meetings, plays and other activities

14. Use of personal computers for word processing and educational games, and occasional use of the library's audiovisual equipment (film projectors, overhead projectors, etc.) for programs in the library

15. A library column in the local homeschooling newsletter, highlighting programs, services, book reviews, books and other materials of special interest, new books

16. Excellent reader's advisory service: help in finding appropriate materials, knowledgeable recommendations regarding materials, an interest in their needs

17. Special borrowing privileges such as those extended to teachers (which homeschoolers are): longer loans, use of audiovisual equipment, books on reserve, filmstrips, videos, use of the library's VCRs by reservation

18. A good collection of children's books and materials that represents a core curriculum for people of all ages. Homeschoolers are especially interested in creative materials that stimulate thinking; historical fiction; biographies; and trade books on science, math, and history.

Homeschooling Laws

Homeschooling is now recognized as a legal form of education in every state of the United States and in all provinces of Canada. However, each state and province has its own rules, regulations, compliance standards, reporting and testing requirements, all of them varying greatly from state to state and from province to province. In the United States, the right to home educate is protected by the First and Fourteenth Amendments to the Constitution (the Fourteenth Amendment guaranteeing parental liberty, which includes the upbringing and education of one's children).

At least five states (Montana, Wyoming, Mississippi, Wisconsin, and Missouri) currently have the minimal requirement that homeschoolers submit an annual notice of intent, verifying that instruction will include certain core subjects and cover the same number of days as the public schools. Some states require periodic testing; some states permit families to obtain religious exemptions from compulsory attendance requirements; some states allow home schools to operate as private schools; others require that home schools be approved by the local school superintendent or school board in order to operate within the law. There has been a recent legislative trend toward less state control of home education.

Despite the legality of the home school as an alternative to public education in every state, certain groups continue to oppose homeschooling in state legislatures. A review of court cases over the past few years shows that there are two major issues involved in this opposition. The first is the question of who has control over the education of children. Public school officials who enforce state compulsory attendance regulations often, understandably, hold the belief that, by virtue of their educational background, they know what is best for the children in their school district. This bias makes it difficult for them to approve of home schools and allow them to operate. The second issue involves the financial interests of the local school district, which stands to lose as much as several thousand dollars of state and federal funds each year for each child in the district who does not attend a public school.

Negativity toward homeschoolers is also evidenced by national education organizations, both in their own resolutions and by their opposition in legislatures. For example, the National Education Association, in its 1991–92 resolutions, stated the belief that "home schooling programs cannot provide the student with a comprehensive education experience" (*NEA Today,* September 1991, pp. 17–23). As a result, there have been a significant number of harassment incidents and legal conflicts each year between homeschoolers and their local school districts. To date, many state and federal cases have resulted in court judgments that support the constitutional rights of homeschoolers to educate their children as they see fit. Some of these cases are described in the books listed below.

Parents who are contemplating homeschooling will often seek legal information in the library concerning the rights and regulations set forth by their home state. Legal information is available from a variety of sources and includes historical information, citations of court cases in various states, discussions of parental rights in education, and information on the laws of each state and province.

Most informed writers on homeschooling laws suggest the following to beginning homeschoolers who are researching the educational laws and regulations of a particular state:

1. Join a local or state home school support group. Often they can provide a copy of the current laws, as well as updates on pending legislation. Many state groups are well organized politically and engage in lobbying. Most have telephone trees in order to keep members informed of changes in the law and other happenings throughout the state.

2. Write to the state Department of Education and request a copy of the state's homeschooling law and any forms that must be submitted. Many states now include homeschooling regulations on their Web sites. Laws concerning homeschooling vary greatly from state to state and province to province. Inquire about the

application process, the types of certification required (if applicable), record keeping, testing and evaluation, and curriculum (objectives, scope, etc.). In some states, homeschoolers may obtain copies of the curriculum for each grade level from their local school district. A growing number of public school districts offer independent study programs that can be used by home-schooled children. Some states require homeschoolers to apply for private school status in order to educate their own children. Many states, as well as the province of Alberta, require periodic standardized testing.

3. Join the Home School Legal Defense Association—an organization that provides low-cost, high-quality legal defense to home educators for any problem involving their right to home school their children. A bimonthly newsletter keeps members informed on legal issues.

Following is a short bibliography of books that include significant information on the history of homeschooling law and parents' rights in education. Also included are several Web sites that summarize the laws of each state and province.

Books

Deckard, Steve. *Home Schooling Laws and Resources Guide for All Fifty States,* 8th ed. Ramona, Calif.: Vision Publishing for S. Deckard, 1996.

Gorder, Cheryl. *Home Schools: An Alternative,* 4th ed. Mesa, Ariz.: Blue Bird Publishing, 1996.

Kaseman, M. Larry, and Susan D. Kaseman. *Taking Charge Through Home Schooling: Personal and Political Empowerment.* Stoughton, Wis.: Koshkonong Press, 1990.

Klicka, Christopher J. *The Right to Home School: A Guide to the Law on Parents' Rights in Education.* Durham, N.C.: Carolina Academic Press, 1995.

Wade, Theodore E. Jr. *The Home School Manual: Plans, Pointers, Reasons, and Resources,* 6th ed., updated. Bridgman, Mich.: Gazelle Publications, 1996.

Whitehead, John W., and Alexis Irene Crow. *Home Education: Rights and Reasons.* Wheaton, Ill.: Crossway Books, 1993.

Web Sites

American Homeschool Association
http://www.home-ed-press.com/HSRSC/hsrsc_lws.rgs.html

> Provides links to homeschooling laws in all fifty states.

The Homeschool Connection
http://frontpage.inet-images.com/hsconnection/proservices.htm

> Detailed summaries of state laws. International laws section (including those for Canadian provinces) was under construction at the time this book was written.

Home School Legal Defense Association
http://www.hslda.org

> Includes statewide organizations and laws for each state presented in a detailed, easy-to-read chart, media releases, and up-to-date legal information.

Sample Programs
and Services

Alexandrian Public Library
115 W. Fifth Street
Mount Vernon, IN 47620
Phone: (812) 838-3286
Fax: (812) 838-9639
E-mail: apl@comsource.net (put "Anne Cottrell" in subject field)
Contact person: Anne Cottrell, Youth Services Coordinator

Special services provided for homeschoolers Publishers' catalogs; vertical file of homeschooling-related information; special collection of books and/or other materials; special bibliographies

Description of services A curriculum enrichment collection is provided for use by teachers, homeschoolers, and parents. Homeschoolers meet in the library each week as a group to use the library's resources. A local homeschooling group uses the meeting rooms each month for organizational meetings. Tours of the library are available upon request.

Special programs provided The homeschoolers use a meeting room each month for a young adult book discussion group they facilitate. The younger siblings meet in another meeting room at the same time for a program planned and presented by the library's children's department staff.

Brown County Library
515 Pine Street
Green Bay, WI 54301-5194
Phone: (920) 448-4381
Contact person: Clare Kindt

Special services provided for homeschoolers Library orientation; vertical file of homeschooling-related information

Description of services The Children's Library has a pamphlet file with materials of special interest to families who home school. Included are bibliographies about homeschooling, state regulations and newsletter information. Names of contact persons for the local homeschoolers support group is available in the "ready reference file" at the Children's Library desk. Through the local support group, a large art display is featured in the Children's Library once a year.

Special programs provided In September, using the newsletter of the local homeschool support group, the Children's Library invites the homeschooling families to the library for a program/tour called "How Can We Help You?" A tour and hands-on experience with an automated catalog and other technologies are part of the program for the adults and older children. Emphasis is given to applying for library cards, explaining services available, and improving reference skills. Younger children are invited to a story time led by a children's services staff member during the tour.

The children's services staff has conducted an in-service program on the subject of homeschooling, its impact on their time and materials, and their response to the special needs of this population. They determined the number of people in their community who have chosen to home school and discussed how the library might better meet their needs. In addition, they revised their "Service to Schools" policy in the following manner in order to include homeschool families: "The children's collection is designed to complement the resources of schools and home-based education systems."

Cambridge Public Library
449 Broadway
Cambridge, MA 02138
Phone: (617) 349-4038
Fax: (617) 349-4028

E-mail: dmark@ci.cambridge.ma.us
Contact person: Daryl Mark

Special services provided for homeschoolers Library orientation; vertical file of homeschooling-related information; special collection of books and/or other materials

Description of services A resource directory, developed by home-schoolers and the librarian, is housed in the library's parenting collection. It includes information on state laws and regulations, resources for information on homeschooling and supplies, booklists, names of contact persons, and a list of suggestions for field trips in the area.

Special programs provided The library has a monthly meeting for homeschoolers which focuses on available library materials on selected topics. A branch of the library has supplied meeting space for a homeschoolers' theater group, and meeting space and publicity have been provided for a Homeschoolers' Science Fair. The homeschoolers have been wonderful library supporters and users!

Clearwater Public Library System
100 N. Osceola Avenue
Clearwater, FL 34615
Phone: (813) 462-6800, ext. 242
Fax: (813) 462-6420
E-mail: mmcgrath@public.lib.ci.clearwater.fl.us
Contact person: Marsha McGrath

Special services provided for homeschoolers Volunteer program; library orientation; display area; publishers' catalogs; vertical file of homeschooling-related information; special collection of books and/or other materials; special bibliographies

Description of services The library offers tours, library orientation, and speakers at homeschoolers' meetings, meeting room space for the homeschoolers' 4-H group, display space for science fair projects, volunteer opportunities for teens, puppeteers, and special programs. Homeschoolers are included in the library system's youth services brochure.

Special programs provided All programs offered by the library are open to homeschool students. Because they don't have a rigid schedule, volunteer opportunities are available during the day (such as during preschool story time) or during the first week of summer when public school students are not available.

Eureka Public Library
202 S. Main
Eureka, IL 61530
Phone: (309) 467-2922
Fax: (309) 467-3527
E-mail: eure@darkstar.rsa.lib.il.us
Contact persons: Nancy Scott, Director
　　　　　　　　Pam Binkley, Children's Librarian

Special services provided Vertical file of homeschooling-related information; special collection of books and/or other materials

Description of services The Parent/Teacher collection includes several books on homeschooling, sets of books for teaching values and subjects, and related material for parents and teachers. A vertical file folder in the children's reference collection contains information on how to home school, various curriculum packages, and resources. A homeschool manual from the Christian Home Educators contains information specific to Illinois laws. Special assistance is available from the children's librarian, who will help locate materials, give reader's advisory service, refer individuals to home education organizations, and provide programs for homeschool groups. The library director provides similar information for anyone who asks.

Hutchinson Public Library
901 N. Main
Hutchinson, KS 67501
Phone: (316) 663-5441
Fax: (316) 663-1215
E-mail: juliet@hplsck.org
Contact person: Julie Tomlianovich

Special services provided for homeschoolers Library orientation; display area; bulletin board; publishers' catalogs; vertical file of homeschooling-related information; special collection of books and/or other materials

Description of services   The library makes sure to include homeschoolers in all publicity for library programs. Local homeschooling newsletters have proven to be an excellent way for both organizations to get together.

Special programs provided   The library tries to treat homeschoolers in the same way as conventional schools, classes, and teachers. They participate in all programs. An annual workshop for homeschoolers acquaints them with all the library has to offer.

Redmond Library (King County Library System)
15810 NE 85th Street
Redmond, WA 98052
Phone: (425) 885-1861
Contact person: Colleen Brazil or Pamela LaBorde

Special services provided for homeschoolers   Volunteer program; library orientation; display area; vertical file of homeschooling-related information

Description of services   The library provides community service volunteer opportunities. Display space is available upon request.

Special programs provided   Book discussion groups are provided for both children and teens; occasional programs are offered on the legalities of homeschooling; library tours are offered.

Rhinelander District Library
106 N. Stevens Street
Rhinelander, WI 54501
Phone: (715) 365-1050
Fax: (715) 365-1076
E-mail: rhinlib@newnorth.net
Contact person: Kris Adams Wendt, Children's Librarian

Special services provided for homeschoolers   Library orientation; publishers' catalogs; vertical file of homeschooling-related information; special collection of books and/or other materials; free use of meeting room

Description of services   The library provides linkage between new homeschool families and established mentors. Homeschoolers receive the same six-week borrowing privileges that are extended to teachers in traditional classrooms. Rather than viewing home school families as a separate species, this library chooses to regard them as another customer user group with specific needs. A strong tradition of service to schools and the ability to design department policies to fit changing customer needs has enabled the library to maintain a very positive relationship with the home-schooled population.

Special programs provided   Homeschoolers are welcome to join in any of the programs offered for children of all ages. Homeschool support groups frequently meet at the library and use the facility to conduct programs related to their curriculum. The library provides materials and equipment as needed.

PART II

Directory of Resources

The number of homeschooling organizations throughout the United States and Canada continues to grow along with the rising number of homeschooling families. The lists of organizations that follow represent a large portion of the national homeschooling organizations and a selection of state and regional associations comprised of those that responded to a questionnaire that was sent out in preparation for this book. A more complete list of organizations in a specific state can be obtained by contacting the state Department of Education (listed here by state). For further information regarding regional and local Canadian organizations, contact the Association of Canadian Home-Based Education, or visit their Web site (see listing below).

National Homeschooling Organizations

United States

Alliance for Parental Involvement in Education (ALLPIE)
P.O. Box 59
East Chatham, NY 12060-0059
Office: 29 Kinderhook Street, Chatham, NY 12060-0059
Phone: (518) 392-6900
E-mail: allpie@taconic.net
Web site: http://www.croton.com/allpie
Contact persons: Seth Rockmuller
                 Katharine Houk

Religious affiliation   None

Materials/services provided   Annual conference; book catalog; workshops; lending library; newsletters: *Options in Learning* and *New York State Home Education News* (contains information of interest to homeschoolers in New York); parent support; educational enrichment materials; homeschooling information/publications

Statement   ALLPIE is "a nonprofit organization which assists and encourages parental involvement in education, wherever that education takes place: in public school, in private school, or at home."

Alternative Education Resource Organization (AERO)
417 Roslyn Road
Roslyn Heights, NY 11577
Phone: (516) 621-2195 or 1-800-769-4171
Fax: (516) 625-3257
E-mail: jmintz@igc.apc.org
　　　　jmintz@acl.nyit.edu
　　　　jmintz@igc.acp.com
Contact person: Jerry Mintz

Materials/services provided   Newsletter: *Aerogramme*

Statement   "AERO is sponsored by the School of Living—a fifty-nine-year-old nonprofit organization. Founder Jerry Mintz has worked with hundreds of alternative schools and homeschool programs and is an expert on educational alternatives. AERO helps people who want to start new community schools, public or private, or change existing schools and provides information to people interested in homeschooling their children or finding private or public alternative schools."

American Homeschool Association
P.O. Box 3142
Palmer, AK 99645-3142
Phone: (907) 746-1336
Fax: (907) 746-1336
E-mail: AHAonline@aol.com
Web site: http://www.home-ed-press.com/AHA/aha.html

Religious affiliation   None

Materials/services provided   Homeschooling information/publications; newsletter: *AHA Networker;* online newsletter: *The AHA Online Newsletter*

Statement   "The American Homeschool Association is a free service organization supporting the continued growth of the homeschooling movement by providing communications and networking for homeschooling families and anyone interested in home education." Networking is offered through three E-mail listservs: the Primary Networking List; the Library Outreach List; and the Support Groups List. "The AHA maintains Homeschooling Resource Files with active links to many recommended resources, along with downloadable files for Web sites, electronic networks, and all fifty states."

Home School Legal Defense Association
P.O. Box 3000
Purcellville, VA 20132
Phone: (540) 338-5600
Fax: (540) 338-2733
E-mail: mailroom@hslda.org
Web site: www.hslda.org

Materials/services provided   Parent support; referral; curriculum resources; networking (homeschooling families and other agencies); legislation monitoring; homeschooling information; annual convention; newsletter; legal counseling and defense

Statement   "The Home School Legal Defense Association is a nonprofit advocacy organization established to defend and advance the constitutional right of parents to direct the education of their children and to protect family freedoms. For an annual membership fee, families may join the association, becoming co-advocates with us." HSLDA represents member families in legal proceedings, prosecutes federal civil rights actions for members, tracks federal legislation affecting home schooling and parents' rights, and provides advocacy in state legislatures upon request of state homeschooling organizations.

Homeschool Support Network
P.O. Box 708
Gray, ME 04039
Phone: (207) 657-2800
Fax: (207) 657-2404
E-mail: hsn@outrig.com
Web site: http://outrig.com/hsn/

Materials/services provided   Information packs; regional conferences throughout the country; local book fairs and seminars; magazine: *Home Educator's Family Times*

Statement   "Homeschool Support Network is a nonprofit service organization working to encourage parents who have chosen to educate their own children." The Web site offers an online version of the magazine, an online help desk, and information on how to contact the organization.

Latter-Day Saint Home Educators' Association
2770 S. 1000 West
Perry, UT 84302
Phone: (801) 723-5355
Fax: (801) 723-3307
Contact person: Joyce Kinmont

Religious affiliation   Church of Jesus Christ of Latter-Day Saints (Mormon)

Materials/services provided   Parent support; curriculum; referral; curriculum resources; networking (homeschooling families); homeschooling information; annual convention; newsletter: *A Call to Closeness*

Statement   "The Latter-Day Saint Home Educators' Association has no official connection with the LDS Church. The LDS-HEA provides support and information to parents, particularly those outside of Utah, who wish to take full responsibility for the education of their children."

The Moore Foundation
Box 1
Camas, WA 98607
Phone: (360) 835-5500
Fax: (360) 835-5392
Phone (orders): (360) 835-2736
E-mail: moorefnd@pacifier.com
Web site: www.caslink.com/moorefoundation

Religious affiliation   Independent (Note: the Moores are Seventh-day Adventists)

Materials/services provided   Parent support; curriculum materials; educational enrichment materials (games, software, flashcards, etc.); homeschooling information/publications; newsletter: *Moore Report International*

Statement   "The Moore Foundation is a nonprofit educational and research organization. It primarily serves educators in public, private, and home schools. It is not a policy-making body. It imposes no stand on religion, politics, nor 'methods' on its clients or supporters. It does not compete with state support groups, but offers service to anyone requesting assistance." The Moore Formula stresses relaxed teaching and emphasizes the combination of study, manual work, and home and/or community service

Muslim Home School Network and Resource (MHSNR)
P.O. Box 803
Attleboro, MA 02703
Phone: (508) 226-1638
E-mail: MHSNR@aol.com
Web site: http://www.ici.net/cust_pages/taadah/taadah.html

Religious affiliation   Muslim

Materials/services provided   Parent support; curriculum resources; other educational resources; networking (homeschooling families); newsletter: *Al-Madrasah Al-Ula*

Statement   "The mission of MHSNR is: 1. To provide the Muslim home schooling community with as many choices and resources as possible. 2. To create and maintain networking resources for Muslim home schooling families. No matter where a Muslim home schooling family resides, we want to insure that they never feel alone." The Web site lists regional and local Muslim support groups and offers online support as well. Membership includes twelve issues of the newsletter and various discounts on books and other homeschooling materials.

National Association for the Legal Support of Alternative Schools (NALSAS)
P.O. Box 2823
Santa Fe, NM 87504-2823
Phone: (505) 471-6928
Fax: (505) 474-3220
Contact persons: Ed Nagel, Coordinator
                 Mary Warner

Religious affiliation   None

Materials/services provided   Parent support; referral; other educational resources; networking (other agencies); homeschooling information; other services (dealing with officials and authorities; advising and defending parents); semi-annual newsletter: *Tidbits*

Statement   "NALSAS is a national information and legal service center designed to research, coordinate, and support legal actions involving nonpublic educational alternatives. NALSAS helps interested persons/organizations locate/evaluate/create viable alternatives to traditional schooling approaches."

National Association of Catholic Home Educators
6102 Saints Hill Road
Broad Run, VA 22014
Phone: (540) 349-4314
E-mail: mdwrmw@juno.com
Contact persons: Bill and Lisanne Bales

Religious affiliation   Catholic

Materials/services provided   Parent support; referral; networking (homeschooling families); homeschooling information; annual convention; newsletter

National Center for Home Education
P.O. Box 3000
Purcellville, VA 20134
Phone: (540) 338-7600
Fax: (540) 338-9333
E-mail: HSLDA@HSLDA.org
Web site: http://www.hslda.org
Contact person: Christopher Klicka, Executive Director

Materials/services provided   Referral; networking (homeschooling families and other agencies); legislation monitoring; homeschooling information; newsletter

Statement   "Founded in 1990 by the Home School Legal Defense Association, the National Center for Home Education assists state home schooling organizations and their leaders by disseminating legislative information related to homeschooling. HSLDA fully funds the National Center and makes its services available free to state home school leaders." The Congressional Action Program, established in 1992, trains Washington D.C. area homeschoolers to lobby for home school–related issues and has a network of members in the 435 congressional districts who lobby their congressmen regarding pending legislation. It also serves as a clearinghouse of major home school research, producing position papers and analyses of federal issues relevant to home education.

National Challenged Homeschoolers Associated Network
5383 Alpine Road, SE
Olalla, WA 98359
Phone: (253) 857-4257
Fax: (253) 857-7764
E-mail: NATHANEWS@aol.com
Contact person: Tom Bushnell

Religious affiliation   Christian

Materials/services provided   Parent support; curriculum; referral; curriculum resources; other educational resources; networking (homeschooling families); homeschooling information; newsletter *(The NATHHAN News);* directory; family camp; resource room; parent learning center

Statement   "NATHHAN is a Christian, nonprofit, network of families encouraging each other in the area of teaching our children."

National Coalition of Alternative Community Schools (NCACS)
P.O. Box 15036
Santa Fe, NM 87506
Phone: (505) 474-4312
Fax: (505) 474-4312
Contact person: Ed Nagel, National Office Manager

Religious affiliation   Nonsectarian

Materials/services provided   Parent support; referral; curriculum resources; other educational resources; networking (homeschooling families and other agencies); legislation monitoring; homeschooling information; annual convention; newsletter; publishes *Directory of Alternative Schools*

Statement   "NCACS supports alternative educational choices, facilitates communication and exchanges among members, and provides information to members and the general public." The organization also supports "educational processes which develop tools and skills for working toward social justice."

National Home Education Research Institute
P.O. Box 13939
Salem, OR 97309
Phone: (503) 364-1490
Fax: (503) 364-2827
E-mail: mail@nheri.org
Web site: http://www.nheri.org
Contact person: Brian D. Ray, Ph.D.

Religious affiliation   None

Materials/services provided   Referral; homeschooling information; newsletter: *Home School Researcher;* research projects; consultation

Statement   "The mission of NHERI is threefold: 1. To produce high-quality research on home education; 2. To serve as a clearinghouse of research for home educators, researchers, and policy makers; 3. To educate the public concerning the findings of all research on home education." NHERI offers research reports, a quarterly journal, and consultation.

National Homeschool Association
P.O. Box 290
Hartland, MI 48353-0290
Voice mail: (513) 772-9580

Religious affiliation   None

Materials/services provided   Referral; networking (homeschooling families); homeschooling information; annual conference; information packet; Homeschoolers' Travel Directory

Statement   "The National Homeschool Association exists to advocate individual choice and freedom in education, to serve those families who chose to homeschool, and to inform the general public about home education."

The Rutherford Institute
P.O. Box 7842
Charlottesville, VA 22906-7482
Phone: (804) 978-3888
Fax: (804) 978-1789
E-mail: tristaff@rutherford.org
Web site: www.rutherford.org

Religious affiliation Nonsectarian

Materials/services provided Parent support; homeschooling information; newsletter

Statement "The Rutherford Institute is a nonprofit legal and educational organization dedicated to preserving and defending religious and civil liberties." It is "an international organization of attorneys and concerned citizens who fight in and out of the courts for religious liberty, family rights, and the sanctity of human life, in addition to handling media relations and providing educational programs to teach people about their religious freedoms."

Canada

Association of Canadian Home-Based Education (ACHBE)
P.O. Box 476
Iroquois Falls, Ontario P0K 1G0 Canada
E-mail: homeschool-ca-org-owner@flora.org
Web site: http://www.flora.org/homeschool-ca/achbe/index.html

Religious affiliation None

Materials/services provided Parent support; networking (homeschooling families); homeschooling information; newsletter (future); mailing list

Statement An online national homeschooling organization with branches in each province, "ACHBE is committed to providing support, advice and information to individuals and organizations. Acting as a special interest group nationally and regionally, ACHBE will help to protect the rights of all Canadians to educate their children at home. ACHBE has no political or religious affiliations." The mailing list provides "a forum for Canadians to discuss legal and regulatory issues affecting the rights of parents to make educational choices for their children." Web site includes links to resources about standardized testing and a list of contact people (with E-mail addresses) for each province.

Natural Life
R R 1
St. George, Ontario N0E 1N0 Canada
Fax: (519) 448-4411
E-mail: natural@life.ca
Web site: http://www.netroute.net/altpress/ds
Contact person: Wendy Priesnitz

Religious affiliation   Nonsectarian

Materials/services provided   Referral; curriculum resources; other educational resources; networking (other agencies); homeschooling information

Statement   Formerly known as the Canadian Alliance of Home Schoolers, Natural Life has provided "information about deschooling to Canadian families since 1979. Founder Wendy Priesnitz, author of the bestselling book *School Free,* is considered Canada's deschooling expert."

State, Regional, and Provincial Organizations

United States

ALABAMA

Alabama Home Educators Network
3015 Thurman Road
Huntsville, AL 35805
Phone: (205) 534-6401
E-mail: KaekaeB@aol.com

Area of influence   Statewide

Religious affiliation   None

Services provided   Parent support; other educational resources; networking; homeschooling information

Statement   "This is a new, just getting off the ground state network. We are inclusive and open to all styles of homeschooling."

Alabama State Department of Education
Cassandra Ramey, Homeschooling Office
50 N. Ripley Street
Montgomery, AL 36130-2102
Phone: (334) 242-8165
E-mail: cramey@sdenet.alsde.edu

ALASKA

Alaska Private & Home Educators Association
P.O. Box 141764
Anchorage, AK 99514
Web site: http://www.aphea.org

Area of influence Statewide

Religious affiliation None

Services provided Parent support; referral; networking (homeschooling families); legislation monitoring; homeschooling information; annual convention; newsletter

Statement Run by a seven-member Board of Directors, APHEA acts as liaison between private education and the Alaska legislature. Members receive regular bulletins regarding pertinent legislation and Department of Education activities. The association also provides referral to private schools or homeschool groups; seminars around the state; information on scholarship programs and educational opportunities; and a newsletter: *APHEA Network News.* The Web site includes a list of Alaska home-school support groups, including contact people, phone, and E-mail address for each.

Alaska State Department of Education
Education Support Services Division
801 W. Tenth Street, Suite 200
Juneau, AK 99801-1894
Phone: (907) 465-2875
        (907) 465-2800 (General information)
Web site: http://www.educ.state.ak.us/

ARIZONA

Arizona Families for Home Education
P.O. Box 4661
Scottsdale, AZ 85261-4661
Phone: (602) 443-0612 (Phone number may change periodically)
E-mail: afhe@primenet.com
Web site: http://www.primenet.com/~afhe

Area of influence Statewide

Religious affiliation Independent support groups are multiple faiths; some have no affiliation

Services provided Referral to independent support groups; curriculum resources; legislation monitoring; homeschooling information; annual convention; newsletter: *Arizona Home Education Journal* (bimonthly); regional workshops; promotion and assistance of independent support groups; public relations; information packet available

Statement "The objectives of AFHE include: educating homeschool families, educators, the public and elected officials on the legal requirements as well as the merits of home-based education; monitoring state and national legislation affecting home schooling; and maintaining the rights of parents and promoting the least restrictive laws and policies pertaining to home schooling."

Arizona Department of Education
1535 W. Jefferson Street, Room 427
Phoenix, AZ 85007
Attn: Trudy Rogers, Alternative Education
Phone: (602) 542-4361 (General information)
Web site: http://www.ade.state.az.us/

ARKANSAS

Coalition of Arkansas Parents
P.O. Box 192455
Little Rock, AR 72219
Phone: (501) 565-6583
Fax: (501) 565-5539
E-mail: jtgreen@athena.ualr.edu
Web site: http://bucket.ualr.edu/~sort/cap.html
Contact person: Ann Green, Executive Director

Area of influence Statewide

Religious affiliation None

Services provided Parent support; curriculum; referral; curriculum resources; other educational resources; networking; legislation monitoring; homeschooling information; newsletter

Statement   "CAP networks with other local, regional and statewide organizations when they focus on educational issues. We have a speakers bureau, issue press releases as appropriate, and conduct training sessions for individuals who wish to participate in the political process. Participation in CAP is open to anyone regardless of race, creed, political or religious affiliation. Respect for privacy is assured (i.e., no information given to CAP will be shared with anyone, including the mailing list)."

Arkansas Department of Education
Arch Ford Education Building
Four Capitol Mall
Little Rock, AR 72201-1071
Phone: (501) 682-4475 (General information)

CALIFORNIA

The California Home=Education Conference
P.O. Box 231324
Sacramento, CA 95823-0405
Phone: (916) 391-4942 (Barbara)
        (916) 927-6181
Fax: (916) 391-4942
E-mail: barbara@chec95.com
Web site: http://www.chec95.com
Contact persons: Barbara David
                 Claudia Camuso

Area of influence   Statewide

Religious affiliation   None

Services provided   Annual convention; directory of speakers for home-school conferences

Statement   "The California Home=Education Conference provides a neutral, single-agenda forum for families who have taken charge of their own learning; where they may explore new ideas, engage in discussions with peers, discover creative resources, examine teaching techniques, and share common experiences. Though our slant is distinctly toward the 'unschooling' or 'child-led' approach as opposed to the structured, classroom style, we have but one agenda: to help families find the way homeschooling works best for them."

California Homeschool Network
P.O. Box 44
Vineburg, CA 95487-0044
Phone: 1-800-327-5339
E-mail: CHNmail@aol.com
Web site: http://www.comenius.org/chn/contact.htm

Services provided   Parent support; networking; legislation monitoring; homeschooling information; bimonthly newsletter: *CHNews*. A network of CHN local contacts is available throughout California to answer individual questions. Also available are a video: *Homeschooling Stands to Reason;* two homeschooling guides: *CHN Support Group Guide* and *Homeschooling in California: Our Rights, Our Laws, and Our Children;* and the California Information Packet.

Christian Home Educators Association of California (CHEA)
P. O. Box 2009
Norwalk, CA 90651-2009
Shipping address: 12440 E. Firestone Boulevard, Suite 1008
                  Norwalk, CA 90650
Phone: (562) 864-2432
Fax: (562) 864-3747
E-mail: cheaofca@aol.com
Web site: http://www.cheaofca.org

Area of influence   Statewide

Local affiliates   Local autonomous support groups

Religious affiliation   Christian

Services provided   Referral; curriculum resources; networking; legislation monitoring; homeschooling information; annual convention; members' magazine; local conventions; other publications

Statement   CHEAC "promotes private Christian home education as an outstanding educational opportunity and provides information, training, and support to the home school community." A six-minute informational phone message describes services and literature and current home education events (1-800-564-2432).

The Home School Association of California
P.O. Box 2442
Atascadero, CA 93423-2442
Phone: (888) HSC-4440
E-mail: info@hsc.org
Web site: http://www.hsc.org
Contact persons: Melissa Hatheway (707) 763-6747
                 Mary Griffith (916) 784-8193

Area of influence   Statewide

Local affiliates   County contacts

Religious affiliation   None

Services provided   Parent support; referral; curriculum resources; other educational resources; networking (homeschooling families and other agencies); legislation monitoring; homeschooling information; annual convention; newsletter: *California Homeschooler;* publications; campouts

Statement   "The Homeschool Association of California honors the diversity of homeschoolers, supports and promotes the entire spectrum of homeschooling, provides information, monitors and influences legislation, and offers opportunities for families to get together."

California Department of Education
P.O. Box 944272
721 Capitol Mall
Sacramento, CA 94244-2720
Phone: (916) 657-2451 (General information)
        (916) 657-2453
E-mail: cpirillo@cde.ca.gov
Contact person: Carolyn Pirillo, Deputy General Counsel, Legal Office

COLORADO

Christian Home Educators of Colorado
3739 East Fourth Avenue
Denver, CO 80206
Phone: (303) 388-1888 (Info hotline)
        (303) 393-6587
Web site: http://www.chec.org

Area of influence Statewide

Religious affiliation Christian

Services provided Curriculum resources; legislation monitoring; home-schooling information; annual conference; public relations; news magazine: *Homeschool Update* (quarterly); Homeschool Hotline service; information packet

Statement "CHEC is an organization dedicated to promoting home schooling in the state of Colorado. Our primary vehicle is an annual statewide conference, but we also use (our) Web site and quarterly news magazine. CHEC is also active in monitoring local legislative issues in the State of Colorado, and works with local Colorado support groups to distribute information which benefits homeschoolers." Web site includes Colorado home school law.

Colorado Home Education Association
4008 Dogwood Court
Loveland, CO 80538

Area of influence Statewide

Services provided Phone tree; newsletter; legislative watching; referrals to local groups

Statement CHEA's purpose is: "to promote and encourage local support groups; to promote quality education; and to promote public acceptance (of homeschooling)."

Colorado Home Educators' Association
c/o Sharyl Macleod
3043 South Laredo Circle
Aurora, CO 80013
Phone: (303) 441-9938
Fax: (303) 766-2696
E-mail: chea@tms-co.com
        olivia@purplemtn.com
Contact person: Olivia C. (Contact person and address change—
        phone number does not)

Area of influence Statewide

Religious affiliation Nonsectarian

Services provided Parent support; referral; networking (home-schooling families and other agencies; newsletter; other services (spelling bee, Odyssey of the Mind, geography bee)

Statement "The purpose of the organization is to promote home education by producing and disseminating a state newsletter, promoting and encouraging local support groups, promoting public awareness and acceptance of home education, promoting favorable legislation and legal action, and promoting sound home education programs."

Concerned Parents of Colorado
P.O. Box 547
Florissant, CO 80816-0547
Phone: (719) 748-8360
Fax: (719) 748-8360
E-mail: Treonelain@aol.com
Web site: to be announced
Contact person: Treon Goossen

Area of influence Statewide/National

Religious affiliation Nonsectarian

Services provided Legislation monitoring; homeschooling information; fax service by subscription

Statement "CPC was formed for the purpose of writing and passing the current homeschool statute in Colorado. CPC monitors the state legislature and gets pertinent information to groups and individuals via fax and (soon) E-mail. CPC also tracks federal issues relating to family and home education."

Colorado State Office of Education
201 E. Colfax Avenue
Denver, CO 80203-1799
Phone: (303) 866-6600 (General information)

CONNECTICUT

The Education Association of Christian Homeschoolers (T.E.A.C.H.)
25 Field Stone Run
Farmington, CT 06032
Phone: 1-800-205-7844 (in Connecticut)
Fax: (860) 677-4677
Web site: http://www.tiac.net/users/raysheen/teach/
Contact person: Ray Sheen

Area of influence Statewide (local affiliates)

Religious affiliation Christian

Services provided Parent support; referral; networking (homeschooling families); legislation monitoring; homeschooling information; annual convention; newsletter

Unschoolers Support
22 Wildrose Avenue
Guilford, CT 06437
Phone: (203) 458-7402
E-mail: guiluniv@ct1.nai.net
Contact person: Liz Shosie

Area of influence Statewide

Religious affiliation Nonsectarian

Services provided Parent support; other educational resources; networking (homeschooling families and other agencies); legislation monitoring; homeschooling information; newsletter; skills and information exchange

Statement In addition to activities such as family gatherings for the purpose of support and idea sharing, Unschoolers Support offers a learning exchange mailing list called Connections, which is used by group members to connect with people from all over Connecticut who want to share their knowledge, ideas, goods, services, and activities. The Shosies have started another learning exchange—Guilford University—which is not limited to members of the Unschoolers Support group. Names and phone numbers from the lists are given out upon request.

Connecticut State Department of Education
165 Capitol Avenue
Hartford, CT 06106
Phone: (860) 566-5677 (General information)

DELAWARE

Delaware Home Education Association
1712 Marsh Road, Suite 172
Wilmington, DE 19810
Phone: (302) 475-0574
Fax: (302) 475-0574
E-mail: jcpoe@concentric.net
Contact person: John Poe (Contact person changes every two to three
                years)

Area of influence   Statewide

Religious affiliation   Christian leadership, but all Delaware homeschoolers are welcome

Services provided   Parent support; referral; networking (other agencies);
legislation monitoring; homeschooling information; annual convention

Statement   "We seek to safeguard the right of parents to choose the
education for their children, work in the area of parental rights and
responsibilities, and network home school groups in the state. We encourage the exchange and sharing of information that would benefit
students and parents in the home school community.

Delaware Public Instruction Department
Steven J. Adamowski, Associate Superintendent
Townsend Building
P.O. Box 1402
Dover, DE 19903-1402
Phone: (302) 739-4645

DISTRICT OF COLUMBIA

District of Columbia Public School System
415 Twelfth Street, N.W., Suite 1205
Washington, DC 20004
Phone: (202) 724-4044 (General information)

FLORIDA

Circle Christian School (formerly Florida at Home)
4644 Adanson Street
Orlando, FL 32804-2024
Phone: (407) 740-8877
Fax: (407) 740-8580
E-mail: circle@ao.net

Area of influence   Regional/Statewide

Religious affiliation   Christian

Age levels served   6–18 years

Services provided   Parent support; curriculum; referral; networking; legislation monitoring; homeschooling information; annual convention; newsletter

Statement   "Circle Christian School provides tools and resources to parents so they can make investments of character and academic excellence in the lives of their children."

Florida Parent-Educators Association (FPEA)
P.O. Box 372
Melbourne, FL 32902-0371
Phone: (407) 722-0895
Fax: (407) 725-2090
E-mail: office@fpea.com
Web site: http://www.fpea.com
Contact person: Dave Exley, Association Manager (changes periodically)

Area of influence   Statewide

Religious affiliation   Nonsectarian

Services provided   Parent support; referral; networking (homeschooling families); homeschooling information; annual convention; newsletter; publication: *The Guide to Homeschooling in Florida*

Statement   "FPEA, Florida's largest nonprofit, inclusive association of homeschool families, is member-supported. Its objective is to inform, encourage, and connect parents who home educate their children."

Florida Department of Education
The Capitol, PL-08
Tallahassee, FL 32399
Phone: (904) 488-9968 (General information)

GEORGIA

Georgia Home Education Association
245 Buckeye Lane
Fayetteville, GA 30214
Phone: (770) 461-3657
Fax: (770) 461-9053
E-mail: ghea@mindspring.com
Web site: http://www.ghea.org
Contact person: Ken Patterson

Area of influence   Statewide

Religious affiliation   Christian

Services provided   Parent support; referral; curriculum resources; networking (homeschooling families); legislation monitoring; homeschooling information; annual convention; newsletter

Statement   "Georgia Home Education Association is dedicated to the Biblical commands for parents to train their children."

Georgia Department of Education
2066 Twin Towers
205 Butler Street, S.E.
Atlanta, GA 30334-5010

Phone: (404) 656-2800 (General information)
Web site: http://www.doe.K12.ga.us

Web site lists curriculum and other requirements for homeschoolers, addresses of state and national homeschooling organizations, and some curriculum resources

HAWAII

Hawaii Homeschool Association
P.O. Box 893476
Mililani, HI 96789
E-mail: lti@lava.net
Web site: http://www.lava.net/~lti

Area of influence   Statewide

Religious affiliation   None

Services provided   Parent support; referral; networking (homeschooling families); homeschooling information; newsletter

Statement   "Hawaii Homeschool Association is a support group of homeschooling families who gather for park days, field trips, and other activities. New homeschoolers are welcome."

Hawaii Department of Education
P.O. Box 2360
Honolulu, HI 96804
Phone: (808) 586-3230 (General information)

IDAHO

Idaho Home Educators
Box 1324
Meridian, ID 83680
Phone: (208) 323-0230
Web site: http://netnow.micron.net/~ihs/ (Homeschooling in Idaho)

Area of influence   Statewide

Religious affiliation   None

Services provided Networking (homeschooling families); homeschooling information; annual convention and book fair; used curriculum swap

Statement The organization offers state-level network and support services, trains local support group leaders, and publishes the Idaho State Newsletter in *The Teaching Home* magazine. Web site lists local and regional support groups throughout the state.

Idaho Department of Education
P.O. Box 83720
Boise, ID 83720-0027
Phone: (208) 334-3236
        (208) 334-2281
        1-800-432-4601
Web site: http://netnow.micron.net/~ihs/Reference/forreyqa.html

ILLINOIS

Christian Home Education Coalition
P.O. Box 470322
Chicago, IL 60647
Phone: (773) 278-0673
Fax: (773) 278-0673
E-mail: ILCHEC@aol.com
Contact person: John Thompson or Fran Eaton

Area of influence Statewide

Religious affiliation Christian (nondenominational)

Services provided Parent support; networking; legislation monitoring; homeschooling information; newsletter: *The CHEC Connection*

Statement "Since 1986, CHEC has been involved in lobbying against both state and federal legislation that would be restrictive to home education as well as the family. With state-of-the-art, online computer services, we are able to keep track of all state bills and amendments." The eight-page bimonthly newsletter includes information on bills being considered, as well as other important news and event information. CHEC representatives speak to homeschool support groups throughout the state and at conferences about legislative activity and the work of CHEC.

Illinois State Board of Education
100 N. First Street
Springfield, IL 62777
Phone: (217) 782-4321 (General information)
        (217) 782-2948
Contact person: Chuck Stoeckel, School Approval Section

This office "suggests that parents contact the regional superintendent for their county to obtain necessary information."

INDIANA

Indiana Association of Home Educators
850 N. Madison Avenue
Greenwood, IN 46142
Phone: (317) 859-1202
Fax: (317) 859-1204
E-mail: iahe@inhomeeducators.org
Web site: http://www.inhomeeducators.org
Contact person: Joyce Johnson, Executive Director

Area of influence   Statewide/Regional

Religious affiliation   Christian

Services provided   Parent support; referral; curriculum resources; other educational resources; networking; legislation monitoring; home-schooling information; annual convention; newsletter: *The IAHE Informer*; handbook: *Home Education in Indiana*; video: *Home-schooling in Action*

Statement   Primary functions of IAHE are: "maintaining visibility as home educators with civil government leaders, influencing the legislative process, and sponsoring seminars for parent education. The IAHE is made up of a volunteer board of directors (five homeschooling couples) and sixteen regional representative couples, who are in direct contact with local support groups.

Indiana Department of Education
Room 229, State House
Indianapolis, IN 46204
Phone: (317) 232-6610 (General information)

An information brochure with the pertinent laws is available.

IOWA

Network of Iowa Christian Home Educators
Box 158
Dexter, IA 50070
Phone: 1-800-723-0438 (in Iowa)
        (515) 830-1614 (outside of Iowa)
E-mail: NICHE@netins.net
Web site: http://www.netins.net/

Area of influence   Statewide

Religious affiliation   Christian

Services provided   Referral; networking; legislation monitoring; home-schooling information; annual convention; newsletter

Statement   "The purpose of NICHE is to provide support and information (including legislative and administrative actions) to home-schooling families in the state of Iowa, using a member newsletter and mailed and/or faxed alerts."

Iowa Department of Education
Grimes State Office Building
Des Moines, IA 50319-0146
Phone: (515) 242-5952 (General information)
Web site: http://www.state.ia.us/educate/depteduc/

KANSAS

Teaching Parents Association
P.O. Box 3968
Wichita, KS 67201
Phone: (316) 945-0810
Fax: (316) 685-1617

E-mail: 103472.447@compuserve.com
Contact person: Jim Farthing, President

Area of influence Regional

Religious affiliation Mostly Evangelical Christian; people of all backgrounds welcome

Services provided Parent support; curriculum; referral; networking (homeschooling families); legislation monitoring; homeschooling information; annual convention; newsletter

Statement "The Teaching Parents Association is the organization of the 1,000-plus homeschooling families in the Wichita/Sedgwick County (Kansas) metro area. TPA's goal is to help families reclaim their rightful place as the primary focus of their children's education by offering information including a monthly newsletter, organizing group classes, holding meetings and an annual convention, and much more."

Kansas State Board of Education
120 S.E. Tenth Avenue
Topeka, KS 66612
Phone: (913) 296-3201 (General information)

KENTUCKY

Christian Educators of Kentucky
691 Howardstown Road
Hodgenville, KY 42748
Phone: (502) 358-9270
Fax: (502) 358-9270
E-mail: kychek@juno.com
Contact persons: Don Woolett
               Joe Adams

Area of influence Statewide

Religious affiliation Christian

Services provided Parent support; referral; networking (homeschooling families); legislation monitoring; homeschooling information; annual convention; newsletter

Statement   The purpose of CHEK is "to support parents who wish to home educate their children."

Kentucky Home Education Association
P.O. Box 81
Winchester, KY 40392-0081
Phone: (606) 744-8562
Contact person: David Lanier (Contact person changes yearly)

Area of influence   Statewide

Services provided   Parent support; referral; curriculum resources; networking; legislation monitoring; homeschooling information; newsletter

Kentucky Department of Education
Melissa Hiles
Home Schools/Private Education
500 Mero Street
Frankfort, KY 40601
Phone: (502) 564-3421
           (502) 564-4770 (General information)

LOUISIANA

Louisiana Department of Education
P.O. Box 94064
Baton Rouge, LA 70804-9064
Phone: (504) 342-4411 (General information)

MAINE

Homeschoolers of Maine
H.C. 62, Box 24
Hope, ME 04847
Phone: (207) 763-4251
Fax: (207) 763-4352
E-mail: homeschl@midcoast.com
Web site: http://members.aol.com/spikefoss/index.html
Contact persons: Ed and Kathy Green

Area of influence   Statewide

Religious affiliation   Christian

Services provided   Parent support; curriculum; referral; curriculum resources; other educational resources; networking (homeschooling families and other agencies); legislation monitoring; homeschooling information; annual convention; newsletter: *The Heart of Home*

Statement   "Homeschoolers of Maine is a Christian ministry dedicated to promoting home education in the State of Maine."

Maine Home Education Association
P.O. Box 421
Popsham, ME 04086
Phone: 1-800-520-0577
Contact person: Ann Cox Halkett (Contact person changes biennially; phone number stays the same)

Area of influence   Statewide

Religious affiliation   None

Services provided   Legislation monitoring; referral; annual convention; newsletter (quarterly); bibliography; resource list

Statement   Maine Home Education Association is a nonprofit, nonsectarian organization that provides information on homeschooling laws in the state of Maine, as well as lists of local support groups around the state and certified teachers available for testing. This relatively new organization will soon offer an annual convention and other services.

Southern Maine Home Education Support Network
76 Beech Ridge Road
Scarborough, ME 04074
Phone: (207) 883-9621
Contact person: Eileen Yoder

Area of influence   Statewide

Religious affiliation   None

Services provided   Parent support; referral; curriculum resources; other educational resources; networking (homeschooling families and other agencies); legislation monitoring; homeschooling information; newsletter

Statement   "SMHESN is eclectic, including families who have chosen a nonschooled or 'unschooling' approach and all the variations an individual or family may choose through replicating school at home. We gather to support each other, to create and share resources. We communicate through a newsletter" (available by donation).

Maine Department of Education
23 State House Station
Augusta, ME 04333-0023
Phone: (207) 287-5922
Contact person: Edwin N. Kastuck, Ph.D.

MARYLAND

Maryland Association of Christian Home Educators
P.O. Box 247
Point of Rocks, MD 21777-0247
Phone: (301) 607-4284
Fax: (301) 607-4284
E-mail: MACHE@juno.com
Contact person: Debbie MacConnell

Area of influence   Statewide

Religious affiliation   Primarily, but not exclusively, Protestant

Services provided   Referral; networking (other agencies); legislation monitoring; homeschooling information; annual convention; newsletter; seminars

Statement   "Maryland Association of Christian Home Educators is an association of home education organizations dedicated to securing and preserving home education liberty in Maryland, resolving conflicts at state and local levels, and connecting homeschoolers with useful resources."

Maryland Home Education Association
9805 Flamepool Way
Columbia, MD 21045
Phone: (410) 730-0073

Fax: (410) 964-5720
Contact person: Manfred Smith, Coordinator and founder

Area of influence   Statewide

Religious affiliation   None

Services provided   Parent support; referral; curriculum resources; networking (homeschooling families); legislation monitoring; homeschooling information; annual conference; book buying service; Homeschool Starter Kit, Maryland Legal Packet, and other pamphlets and materials

Statement   MHEA was founded in 1980 to serve and support families of all religious, philosophical, and ethnic persuasions. MHEA has been a leading force in Maryland homeschooling legislation. The organization provides members with up-to-date information, long-term service and support, discounts on educational materials, and other services.

North County Home Educators (NCHE)
1688 Belhaven Woods Court
Pasadena, MD 21122-3727
Phone: (410) 437-5109
Fax: (410) 360-7330
E-mail: 210-8942@MCImail.com
Web site: http://members.aol.com/FUNNews/nche.htm
Contact person: Nancy Greer (changes occasionally; information will
               be passed along)

Area of influence   Regional (Anne Arundel County area)

Religious affiliation   Nonsectarian

Services provided   Parent support; networking (homeschooling families); homeschooling information; newsletter

Statement   "NCHE has been established: 1. To provide a network that welcomes all homeschooling families regardless of their religious beliefs or homeschooling methods. 2. To provide opportunities to access services/benefits a single homeschool family could not obtain alone. 3. To provide sources of information covering a range of interests which could be used in a variety of homeschooling programs."

Maryland State Department of Education
200 W. Baltimore Street
Baltimore, MD 21201
Phone: (401) 767-0100 (General information)

MASSACHUSETTS

Massachusetts Home Learning Association
P.O. Box 1558
Marstons Mills, MA 02648
Phone: (508) 420-3673
Fax: (508) 420-2771
E-mail: lisawood@aol.com
Web site: http://northshore.shore.net/~pyghill/mha.htm
Contact person: Elisa Wood

Area of influence   Statewide

Religious affiliation   None

Services provided   Parent support; referral; networking (homeschooling families); legislation monitoring; homeschooling information; newsletter (quarterly); homeschooling introductory kit

Statement   "MHLA is an all-volunteer, parent run communications network for homeschoolers [that is] not affiliated with any political or religious organizations."

Commonwealth of Massachusetts Department of Education
350 Main Street
Malden, MA 02148-5023
Phone: (617) 388-3300 (General information)

MICHIGAN

Heritage Home Educators
c/o Lisa Hodge Kander
2122 Houser
Holly, MI 48442
E-mail: lhkander@tir.com

For newsletter: Dee Morgan
804 Oak Park
Fenton, MI 48430

Area of influence   Regional (currently ten counties; still growing)

Religious affiliation   None

Services provided   Parent support; networking (homeschooling families); newsletter; phone chain

Statement   "Heritage Home Educators is a not-for-profit organization of homeschoolers founded in 1989 to support home educating families in Michigan by providing parents' meetings, family enrichment activities, children's programs and a newsletter. The group is open to families of all faiths and educational philosophies."

Information Network of Christian Homes (INCH)
4934 Cannonsburg Road
Belmont, MI 49306
Phone: (616) 874-5656
Fax: (616) 874-5577
Contact persons: Dennis and Roxanne Smith

Area of influence   Statewide (local affiliates)

Religious affiliation   Christian—nondenominational

Services provided   Legal referral; curriculum resources; networking (homeschooling families); legislation monitoring; homeschooling information; annual convention; newsletter; copublish *The Teaching Home* magazine; information packet; seminars; leadership training for support leaders

Statement   "INCH's mission is to serve families interested or involved in home education by providing the information, resources, and encouragement needed to teach their children at home in Michigan, and to work to ensure the continued freedom to do so."

Older Homeschoolers' Group
9120 Dwight Drive
Detroit, MI 48214-2944

Phone: (313) 331-8406
Contact person: Diane Linn

Area of influence Regional (currently southeast Michigan and Windsor, Ontario)

Religious affiliation Nonsectarian

Services provided Educational resources; networking (homeschooling families); family activities; weekly educational programs

Statement "The OHG is a nonsectarian support group serving homeschooling families with children twelve years and older who live within about an hour's drive of Detroit. Many social, educational, and service opportunities are offered."

Michigan Department of Education
P.O. Box 30008
Lansing, MI 48909
Phone: (517) 373-3324 (General information)

MINNESOTA

Minnesota Association of Christian Home Educators
P.O. Box 32308
Fridley, MN 55432-0308
Phone: (612) 717-9070
E-mail: mache@isd.net
Web site: http://www.mache.org

Area of influence Statewide

Religious affiliation Christian

Services provided Parent support; annual conference; newsletter

Statement "MACHE was formed in 1983 to encourage Christian families in the home education of their children. It is a statewide, facilitating organization for all parents who have chosen to home school." Web site includes current events and information, as well as links to HSLDA, homeschooling magazines, and other state education organizations' home pages.

Minnesota Homeschoolers' Alliance
P.O. Box 23072
Richfield, MN 55423
Phone: (612) 288-9662

Area of influence   Statewide

Religious affiliation   None

Services provided   Parent support; networking (homeschooling families); legislation monitoring; homeschooling information; newsletter; family dances, teen events; workshops; curriculum fairs

Statement   "MHA, founded in 1991, is a statewide, nonprofit, nonsectarian organization committed to encouraging and enabling homeschool families through education, networking opportunities, activity and guidance on homeschooling issues. MHA is committed to fulfilling its mission without discrimination based on race, religion, or educational philosophy."

Children's Families and Learning Department
Capitol Square Building
550 Cedar Street
St. Paul, MN 55101
Phone: (612) 296-6105 (Private alternative programs)
        1-888-234-4939 (toll free) to find out whom to contact

MISSISSIPPI

Home Educators of Central Mississippi
535 Luling Street
Pearl, MS 39208
Phone: (601) 939-5927
Contact person: John Bynum (Contact person changes yearly—will
                provide forwarding address/phone)

Area of influence   Regional (central Mississippi)

Religious affiliation   Christian

Services provided   Parent support; curriculum resources; other educational resources; legislation monitoring; homeschooling information; annual convention; newsletter

Statement   Home Educators of Central Mississippi helps new families get started homeschooling. The group offers two libraries of materials for members' use, plans field trips, publishes a bimonthly newsletter, and holds an annual conference.

Mississippi Home Educators Association
P.O. Box 945
Brookhaven, MS 39601
Phone: (601) 833-9110
Fax: (601) 833-9110
Web site: http://www.mhea.org
Contact person: changes periodically

Area of influence   Statewide

Religious affiliation   Christian

Services provided   Legislation monitoring; homeschooling information; annual convention; annual curriculum fair; information packet available

Statement   "MHEA is a Christian ministry organization that works directly with local support group leaders throughout the state and, therefore, does not accept individual memberships."

Mississippi Department of Education
P.O. Box 771
Jackson, MS 39205
Phone: (601) 359-3513

MISSOURI

Christian Home Educators Fellowship
3345 Fee Fee Road
St. Louis, MO 63044
Phone: (314) 739-8284 (Hawkins)
        (314) 521-8487 (Summers)
Contact persons: Mark and Shawn Hawkins
                 Jon and Candy Summers

Area of influence   Regional

Religious affiliation   Christian

Services provided   Parent support; curriculum resources; networking (homeschooling families and other agencies); legislation monitoring; homeschooling information; annual educators conference/curriculum fair; homeschooler's handbook; regional workshops, many regional activities (fine arts fair, New Homeschoolers Seminar, used book sale, Choir and Band Festival, Speech and Word Festival, etc.); 8th and 12th grade graduation ceremonies; newsletter

Statement   Currently a network of twenty-five support groups located in the St. Louis area and surrounding counties (including some in Illinois), Christian Home Educators Fellowship is still growing.

Families for Home Education
6209 NW Tower Drive
Platte Woods, MO 64151
Phone: (417) 782-8833
E-mail: fhe@microlink.net
Web site: http://www.microlink.net/~fhe/index.htm

Area of influence   Statewide

Religious affiliation   None

Services provided   Legislation monitoring; homeschooling information; annual convention

Statement   "Families for Home Education (FHE) is the state lobbying organization for home educators in the state of Missouri. Its purpose is to protect the inalienable right of the parents of Missouri to teach their own children without state regulation or control. FHE represents and supports all home educators in the state and is not affiliated with any religious or political organization or any special interest group. We work to win support for home education among the general public and before lawmakers and public officials. Closely monitoring legislative activity in the state capitol, through our registered lobbyist, is our most important activity. FHE provides legally accurate information to anyone interested in home education. FHE leadership ties into local networks through the regional directors. FHE also maintains the Legislative Alert Network, an emergency mailing service to support group leaders throughout the state."

Missouri Department of Elementary and Secondary Education
205 Jefferson Street
P.O. Box 480
Jefferson City, MO 65102-0480
Phone: (573) 751-4212 (General information)

MONTANA

Montana Coalition of Home Educators
Box 43
Gallatin Gateway, MT 59730
Phone: (406) 587-6163
E-mail: white@gomontana.com
Web site: http://www4.gomontana.com/white/mche.htm (in progress)
Contact person: Steve White

Area of influence   Statewide

Religious affiliation   None

Services provided   Parent support; referral; networking; legislation monitoring; homeschooling information; annual convention; newsletter

Montana Office of Public Instruction
P.O. Box 202501
Helena, MT 59620-1201
Phone: (406) 444-3095 (General information)

NEBRASKA

Nebraska Christian Home Educators Association
P.O. Box 57041
Lincoln, NE 68505-7041
Phone: (402) 423-4297
Fax: (402) 420-2610
E-mail: nchea@navix.net
Contact persons: Nick and Kathleen Lenzen (Contact family changes
                 periodically)

Area of influence   Statewide

Religious affiliation   Christian

Services provided   Referral (to local support groups); legislation monitoring; homeschooling information; annual convention and curriculum fair; newsletter

Statement   "The NCHEA's mission includes the encouragement and support of Christian families in the education of their children at home in accordance with Biblical principles, the support and advocacy of the rights of Christian parents to home school their children, and the promotion of the benefits of Christian home education."

Nebraska State Department of Education
301 Centennial Mall South
P.O. Box 94987
Lincoln, NE 68509-4987
Phone: (402) 471-2295 (General information)

NEVADA

Northern Nevada Home Schools, Inc.
P.O. Box 21323
Reno, NV 89515
Phone: (702) 852-NNHS
Fax: (702) 849-7808
E-mail: NNHS@aol.com
Contact person: Nancy Ziese (Contact person changes biennially)

Area of influence   Regional

Religious affiliation   None

Services provided   Parent support; referral; networking (homeschooling families); legislation monitoring; homeschooling information; annual convention; newsletter; phone tree; special workshops

Statement   "The purpose of NNHS is to support, encourage, and assist parents and students who have legally chosen the home education option."

Nevada Department of Education
700 E. Fifth Street
Carson City, NV 89701-5096
Phone: (702) 687-9186 (Standards, Curriculum and Assessment
        Director)

NEW HAMPSHIRE

Christian Home Educators of New Hampshire
P.O. Box 961
Manchester, NH 03105
Phone: (603) 569-2343
Web site: http://www.mv.com/ipusers/chenh
Contact person: Lee Button

Area of influence   Statewide

Religious affiliation   Christian

Services provided   Networking (homeschooling families); legislation monitoring; homeschooling information; annual convention and curriculum fair; newsletter

Statement   "As a recognized state organization, CHENH nominates representatives to the Home Education Advisory Council. This group, made up of homeschoolers and education officials, advises the state Commissioner of Education on matters regarding home education. This allows homeschoolers to have a voice in the administrative regulation process."

New Hampshire State Department of Education
101 Pleasant Street
Concord, NH 03301
Phone: (603) 271-3494 (General information)

NEW JERSEY

Education Network of Christian Homeschoolers of New Jersey (ENOCH of New Jersey)
120 Mayfair Lane
Mount Laurel, NJ 08054-3126
Phone: (609) 222-4283
Fax: (609) 222-4282
E-mail: enochnj@uscom.com
Contact person: Carol Parker, Office Manager (Changes every four to
                five years)

Area of influence   Statewide (local support groups)

Religious affiliation   Christian

Services provided Parent support; referral; legislation monitoring; homeschooling information; annual convention; New Jersey Information Packet

Statement "ENOCH's purpose is to provide service and support to Christian home education support groups and home educators within the state of New Jersey."

Unschoolers Network
2 Smith Street
Farmingdale, NJ 07727
Phone: (732) 938-2473
Contact person: Nancy Plent

Area of influence Regional/Statewide

Religious affiliation Nonsectarian

Services provided Parent support; curriculum; referral; networking (homeschooling families and other agencies); legislation monitoring; homeschooling information; annual conference and curriculum fair; newsletter; introductory workshops around the state; Legal Guide available

Statement Unschoolers Network, established in the late 1970s, provides information, curriculum materials, and support to home educators in the state of New Jersey.

Unschooling Support Group of Central New Jersey
150 Folwell Station Road
Jobstown, NJ 08041
Phone: (609) 723-1524
Contact person: Karen Mende-Fridkis (address will change in 1998)

Area of influence Regional

Religious affiliation Nonsectarian

Age levels served 0–12 years

Services provided Parent support; homeschooling information; field trips; newsletter; lending library

Statement   This organization "assists others who have questions about homeschooling. The group meets regularly for activities (for the children) and discussion (for parents)."

New Jersey Department of Education
River View Executive Plaza
CN500 – Bldg. 100
Trenton, NJ 08625-0500
Phone: (609) 292-4469

NEW MEXICO

New Mexico Family Educators
P.O. Box 92276
Albuquerque, NM 87199-2276
Phone: (505) 275-7053
Fax: (505) 466-4462
E-mail: nmfe@juno.com
Web site: http://members.aol.com/nmfamed/homepage.html
        (currently in transition)
Contact persons: Darla McLeod
                Cindy Santillanes (Contact person changes
                annually or biennially)

Area of influence   Statewide

Religious affiliation   None

Services provided   Parent support; referral; curriculum resources; other educational resources; networking (homeschooling families and other agencies); legislation monitoring; homeschooling information; annual convention; newsletter

New Mexico Department of Education
300 Don Gaspar Street
Santa Fe, NM 87501-2786
Phone: (505) 827-6508 (Associate Superintendent of Learning Services)
Web site: http://sde.state.nm.us

NEW YORK

New York State Loving Education at Home (LEAH)
E-mail: NYSLEAH@juno.com
Web site: http://www.leah.org/

Area of influence   Statewide (local chapters in seven regions)

Religious affiliation   Christian

Services provided   Referral; networking (homeschooling families); legislation monitoring; homeschooling information; annual convention; workshops; leadership training

Statement   "LEAH is a statewide not-for-profit ministry providing local support through a network of local chapters" (obtained from Web site). The association serves on the Home Instruction Advisory Group to the New York State Education Department. Publications include a video on homeschooling and a Regulatory and Informational Manual for Homeschooling in New York State. Regional groups listed on Web site.

Tri-County Home Schoolers
P.O. Box 190
Ossining, NY 10562
Phone: (914) 941-5607
E-mail: chofer@croton.com
Web site: http://www.croton.com/home-ed/ *(Tri-County Home
        Schoolers Home Education Bulletin)*

Area of influence   Regional

Statement   The online bulletin includes a calendar of events sponsored by the organization and selected links to parenting resources, education resources, and resources for children. The *Home Education Bulletin* is also available in print (by subscription).

New York State Education Department
Office of Elementary, Middle, Secondary & Continuing Education
Room 875, Education Bldg. Annex
Washington Avenue
Albany, NY 12234
Phone: (518) 474-3879 Home Instruction (Nancy Moore)
        (518) 474-3852 (General information)

NORTH CAROLINA

North Carolinians for Home Education
419 N. Boylan Avenue
Raleigh, NC 27603-1211
Phone: (919) 834-6243
Fax: (919) 834-6241
E-mail: nche@mindspring.com
Contact person: Susan D. Van Dyke

Area of influence   Statewide

Religious affiliation   Nonsectarian

Services provided   Parent support; referral; networking (homeschooling families); legislation monitoring; homeschooling information; annual conference and book fair; newsletter: *The Greenhouse Report*; annual support group leaders conference

Statement   "NCHE was organized in 1984 to support and encourage home educators and to protect the right to freely home educate in North Carolina. NCHE is a representative organization governed by a board of seven officers, elected by all NCHE members, and twelve regional directors, elected by the NCHE members in each region."

North Carolina Division of Non-Public Education
Office of the Governor
Division of Non-Public Education
Rod Helder, Director
530 North Wilmington Street
Raleigh, NC 27604-1198
Phone: (919) 733-4276
Web site: http://www.gov.state.nc.us/dnpe

See page for North Carolina Home School Information (under Types of Non-Public Schools). The site includes charts of enrollment by age, a statewide history, and a summary of homeschool enrollment by year, age, county, and sex. The North Carolina Home School Information packet includes state legal requirements.

NORTH DAKOTA

North Dakota Home School Association
P.O. Box 7400
Bismarck, ND 58507-7400
Phone: (701) 223-4080
E-mail: gailb@wdata.com
Contact person: Gail Biby

Area of influence   Statewide

Religious affiliation   Christian

Services provided   Parent support; referral; curriculum resources; other educational resources; networking (homeschooling families); legislation monitoring; homeschooling information; annual convention; newsletter

North Dakota Department of Public Instruction
State Capitol, 11th Floor
600 East Boulevard Avenue
Bismarck, ND 58505
Phone: (701) 328-2260 (General information)

OHIO

Christian Home Educators of Ohio
430 N. Court Street
Circleville, OH 43113
Phone: (614) 474-3177
Fax: (614) 474-3652
E-mail: cheohome@bright.net
Web site: http://www.cheohome.org
Contact person: Bruce D. Prudy, Executive Director

Area of influence   Statewide

Religious affiliation   Fundamentalist Christian

Services provided   Parent support; curriculum resources; other educational resources; networking (homeschooling families); legislation monitoring; homeschooling information; annual convention; newsletter

Statement   "CHEO serves as a nonprofit organization seeking opportunities to serve the need of home educators in Ohio. Likewise, CHEO seeks opportunities to educate the general public on the viability of home education as compared to public or private education."

Families Unschooling in the Neighborhood (F.U.N.)
3636 Paris Boulevard
Westerville, OH 43081
Phone: (614) 794-2171
E-mail: roy@qn.net
Contact person: Lori Collner

Area of influence   Regional

Religious affiliation   None

Services provided   Parent support; referral; networking (homeschooling families); legislation monitoring; homeschooling information

Statement   "F.U.N. is a diverse, inclusive play group and social network for families who unschool. Participants share an emphasis on child-led learning and eschew approaches utilizing packaged home school curriculums.

Ohio Department of Education
65 S. Front Street, Room 408
Columbus, OH 43215-4183
Phone: (614) 466-3641 (General information)

OKLAHOMA

Home Educators' Resource Organization (HERO) of Oklahoma
4401 Quail Run Avenue
Skiatook, OK 74070-4024
Phone: (918) 396-0108
Fax: Call for number.
E-mail: moyerles@wiltel.net
Web site: http://www.geocities.com/Athens/Forum/3236
Contact person: Leslie Moyer

Area of influence   Statewide (local support groups)

Religious affiliation Nonsectarian

Services provided Parent support; referral networking (homeschooling families and other agencies); legislation monitoring; homeschooling information; annual conference; newsletter; directory of families and affiliated support groups; E-mail list; E-mail discussion group; *Oklahoma Homeschooling Handbook*

Statement "HERO of Oklahoma's purpose is to provide information concerning the many local, state, national, and international educational resources available to Oklahoma home educators. We wish to work with other established networks in Oklahoma to provide information and resources for Oklahoma homeschoolers."

Oklahoma Department of Education
2500 N. Lincoln Boulevard
Oklahoma City, OK 73105-4599
Phone: (405) 521-3301 (General information)

OREGON

The Oregon Christian Home Education Association Network
17985 Falls City Road
Dallas, OR 97338
Phone: (503) 288-1285 (information)
        (503) 787-3512 (personal contact)
E-mail: oceanet@teleport.com
Web site: http://www.teleport.com/~oceanet
Contact persons: Peter and Joyce Padilla

Area of influence Statewide

Religious affiliation Christian

Services provided Parent support; referral; curriculum resources; other educational resources; networking (homeschooling families); legislation monitoring; homeschooling information; newsletter

Statement "OCEANetwork exists to provide support and communication to Christian home education support group leaders, and to make information accessible to support groups and home educators, governing bodies, and the general public. All activities of OCEANetwork shall be consistently and forthrightly Christian."

Oregon Home Education Network
4470 SW Hall Boulevard, #286
Beaverton, OR 97005
Phone: (503) 321-5166 (Voice mail, answered by volunteer parents)
E-mail: Sassenak@msn.com
Web site: http://www.teleport.com/~ohen

Area of influence   Statewide

Religious affiliation   None

Services provided   Parent support; referral; networking (homeschooling families); legislation monitoring; homeschooling information; annual convention; newsletter: *The Oregon Connection;* resource packet

Statement   "OHEN is an inclusive organization dedicated to the support of Oregon's homeschooling families. The organization maintains a growing list of County Contacts to help homeschoolers find resources in their area." Web site includes information regarding contact people in various counties; homeschooling resources; Oregon homeschooling administrative rules; and links to a large number of "Cool Web Sites."

Parents Education Association
P.O. Box 5428
Beaverton, OR 97006
Phone: (503) 693-0724
E-mail: elderdt@aol.com
Web site: http://www.lyonscom.com/peapac
Contact person: Dennis Tuuri

Area of influence   Statewide

Religious affiliation   Reformational Christianity

Services provided   Parent support; legislation monitoring; homeschooling information; newsletter; legislation introduction; Christian analysis of ballot measures

Statement   PEAPAC issues scriptural-based recommendations on ballot measures to be voted on in Oregon, assists in the development and election of pro-home school candidates for the Oregon House and Senate, and lobbies the Oregon House and Senate "from a distinctly Biblical perspective on a wide range of issues that directly affect home schooling." Web site includes information on various bills, committee calendars, and Web sites of various government agencies and politicians in the state of Oregon, as well as art, literature, and government sites.

Oregon State Department of Education
Public Service Building
225 Capitol Street, NE
Salem, OR 97310-0203
Phone: (503) 378-3573 (General information)

PENNSYLVANIA

Maryland/Pennsylvania Home Learners
P.O. Box 67
Shrewsbury, PA 17361
Phone: (717) 993-3603
  (410) 343-1944
Contact person: Eileen Stein or Kathy Schmitt (Contact person
  changes anually)

Area of influence   Regional

Religious affiliation   Nonsectarian

Services provided   Parent support; referral; curriculum resources; other educational resources; networking (homeschooling families); legislation monitoring; homeschooling information; newsletter; field trips and activities

Statement   "MD/PA Home Learners is a support group for homeschooling families and offers information to those who are considering homeschooling. We meet weekly for field trips and/or activities, and parents meet monthly for planning and sharing of resources, concerns, etc."

Pennsylvania Homeschoolers
RR2 – Box 117
Kittanning, PA 16201-9311
Phone: (412) 783-6512
Fax: (412) 783-6852

E-mail: richmans@pahomeschoolers.com
Web site: http://www.pahomeschoolers.com
Contact persons: Howard and Susan Richman

Area of influence   Statewide

Religious affiliation   None

Services provided   Parent support; curriculum; referral; curriculum resources; other educational resources; networking (homeschooling families and other agencies); legislation monitoring; homeschooling information; annual convention; newsletter; yearly group achievement testing service; sponsors advanced placement Internet courses for homeschool students; high school level educational video course lending library; high school diploma program through Pennsylvania Homeschoolers Accreditation Agency

Statement   In addition to the many services listed above, the Richmans have written and edited books that include their own home school experiences, a portfolio of writing by home-schooled students, and a collection of word problems written by children, as well as *Story of a Bill: Legalizing Homeschooling in Pennsylvania*. The organization also offers accreditation under Pennsylvania law for home education diplomas.

Pennsylvania Department of Education
333 Market Street
Harrisburg, PA 17126-0333
Phone: (717) 783-6788 (General information)
Web site: http://www.cas.psu.edu/pde.html

RHODE ISLAND

Rhode Island Guild of Home Teachers
P.O. Box 11
Hope, RI 02831
Phone: (401) 821-7700 (Information line)
Contact person: Brenda (Contact person changes; information line
                phone number does not change)

Area of influence   Statewide (local affiliates)

Religious affiliation   Nonsectarian

Services provided   Homeschooling information; newsletter (lists each chapter's events and local events of interest); annual curriculum fair; information packet

Statement   This organization currently has nine local chapters, each of which plans and runs its own events, as well as (occasionally) a statewide event (such as a geography fair or a spelling bee).

Rhode Island Elementary and Secondary Education Department
255 Westminister Street
Providence, RI 02903
Phone: (401) 277-4600, Ext. 2003 (General information)

SOUTH CAROLINA

South Carolina Association of Independent Home Schools (SCAIHS)
P.O. Box 2104
Irmo, SC 29063-7104
Phone: (803) 551-1003
Fax: (803) 551-5746
E-mail: SCAIHS@aol.com
Web site: http://members.aol.com/SCAIHS/SCAIHS.htm
Contact person: Zan P. Tyler

Area of influence   Statewide

Religious affiliation   Christian (Membership is open to all)

Services provided   Parent support; curriculum counseling; curriculum resources; other educational resources; legislation monitoring; homeschooling information; annual convention; newsletter; teacher training seminars; permanent records; official transcripts, diplomas, graduation ceremony; resource room; special needs and high school programs

Statement   "SCAIHS is a nonprofit, voluntary association of independent home schools. On July 25, 1990, the State of South Carolina incorporated SCAIHS as an organization to coordinate and establish academic standards and to provide support services for independent home schools. On April 8, 1992, the South Carolina General Assembly enacted legislation naming the South Carolina Association of Independent

Home Schools as a legal, alternative source of approval for home-schooling parents."

The South Carolina Homeschool Alliance
E-mail: ConnectSC@aol.com
Web site: http://members.aol.com/Connectsc/support.htm

Area of influence   Statewide

Religious affiliation   N/A

Statement   "SCHA is an Internet information, communication, and support network for South Carolina homeschoolers. SCHA sponsors the South Carolina Homeschooling Web site and the South Carolina Homeschoolers mailing list. SCHA is not affiliated with any state, local, or national homeschooling groups or businesses. To contact SCHA, please E-mail." Web site includes South Carolina homeschooling laws; local support groups, and a list of South Carolina homeschool accountability associations, with information about each one.

South Carolina Department of Education
1429 Senate Street, Room 1006
Columbia, SC 29201
Phone: (803) 734-8500 (General information)

SOUTH DAKOTA

South Dakota Education and Cultural Affairs Department
700 Governors Drive
Pierre, SD 57501-2291
Phone: (605) 773-3134

TENNESSEE

Tennessee Department of Education
Andrew Johnson Tower
710 James Robertson Parkway
Nashville, TN 37243-0375
Phone: (615) 741-2731 (General information)

TEXAS

Southeast Texas Home School Association
4950 FM 1960 W, Suite 297
Houston, TX 77069
Fax: (281) 655-0963
E-mail: Sethsa@ghgcorop.com
Contact person: Jonathan Weidner

Area of influence   Regional

Religious affiliation   Christian

Services provided   Parent support; referral; networking (homeschooling families and other agencies); legislation monitoring; homeschooling information; two annual conventions; newsletter

Statement   "The Southeast Texas Home School Association is a nonprofit Christian service organization established to minister to the homeschooling community in the greater Houston and Southeast Texas area."

Texas Home School Coalition
P.O. Box 6982
Lubbock, TX 79493-6982
Phone: (806) 797-4927
Fax: (806) 797-4629
E-mail: staff@THSC.org
Web site: http://www.THSC.org
Contact persons: Elaine, Jana, or Lyndsay

Area of influence   Statewide

Religious affiliation   Christian

Services provided   Parent support; referral; networking (homeschooling families); legislation monitoring; homeschooling information; annual convention; newsletter; *THS Review Magazine*

Statement   Texas Home School Coalition is dedicated to the preservation of parents' rights to educate their children at home free from government interference.

Texas Education Agency
1701 N. Congress Avenue
Austin, TX 78701-1494
Phone: (512) 463-9716 (Non-Traditional School Accountability &
                        Development)
       (512) 463-9734 (General information)

UTAH

Utah Christian Homeschool Association
P.O. Box 3942
Salt Lake City, UT 84110-3942
Phone: (801) 296-7198 (Voice mail)
E-mail: Winderjr@aol.com

Area of influence   Statewide

Religious affiliation   Interdenominational Christian

Services provided   Parent support; networking (homeschooling families); legislation monitoring; homeschooling information; annual convention; newsletter workshops; support meetings; used book sale

Statement   "The mission of UTCH (pronounced U-Teach) is to provide support, education, and fellowship for Christian parents who have made the decision to educate their children at home."

Utah Home Education Association
P.O. Box 167
Roy, UT 84067
Phone: (888) 887-UHEA
Fax: (801) 728-0956
E-mail: uhea@itsnet.com
Web site: http://www.itsnet.com/~uhea/
Contact person: Brian Smith (Contact person changes every two years)

Area of influence   Statewide

Religious affiliation   None

Services provided   Parent support; referral; networking; homeschooling information; annual convention and curriculum fair; monthly newsletter: *Right at Home*

Statement The UHEA's five basic goals include "encouraging maintenance and improvement of our rights to educate our own children
through support of good legislation, court decisions, and policies established by public school administrators, and to oppose any limita-
tion to these same rights; establishing and maintaining a diplomatic
relationship with state and local school administration; striving to educate the public to the viability of home education; helping families
find educational resources that best meet their children's needs; encouraging educational and social activities to help maintain family
morale." Newsletter includes a detailed list of Utah homeschool support groups and field trips.

Utah State Office of Education
250 E. 500 S.
Salt Lake City, UT 84111
Phone: (801) 538-7500 (General information)

VERMONT

The Resource Center for Homeschooling
RR2, Box 289-C
St. Albans, VT 05478
Phone: (802) 524-9645
Fax: (802) 524-9645
E-mail: shell@together.net
Contact person: Deb Shell

Area of influence Statewide

Religious affiliation Nonsectarian

Age levels served 13–18 years

Services provided Parent support; curriculum; curriculum resources;
networking (homeschooling families); homeschooling information;
annual convention; newsletter

Statement "This organization was formed to help teenage homeschoolers find other like-minded individuals or groups, to promote opportunities for community involvement, internships, apprenticeships,
classes, and socializing. Deb Shell has extensive experience with unschoolers, especially with teens developing resumes, transcripts, and

whatever else may be involved with finding and attending appropriate experiences, including college, job training, and employment."

Vermont Department of Education
120 State Street
Montpelier, VT 05620-2501
Phone: (802) 828-2756 (General information)
        (802) 828-5406
Contact person: Natalie Casco, School Development—Home and
                Independent School Consultant

VIRGINIA

Home Educators Association of Virginia
P.O. Box 6745
Richmond, VA 23230
Phone: (804) 288-1608
Fax: (804) 288-6962
E-mail: HEAV33@aol.com
Web site: http://www.heav.org

Area of influence   Statewide

Religious affiliation   Nonsectarian

Services provided   Parent support; Virginia history curriculum; referral; networking (homeschooling families and other agencies); legislation monitoring; homeschooling information; annual state convention and educational fair; newsletter; regional seminars; support group leader conferences; statewide graduation ceremony; beginner and information packets

Statement   "HEAV serves all homeschoolers and is committed to help parents fulfill their God-given right to educate their own children. We do this through lobbying and legislative efforts, online monitoring of legislation, close networking with the Department of Education, local school boards, and state and national home school and pro-family organizations."

Home Instruction Support Group (HIS)
Rt. 1, Box 878
Bluemont, VA 20135
Phone: (540) 554-2500
Fax: (540) 554-2938
E-mail: Laurelwood@juno.com
Contact person: Mary Ellen

Area of influence Regional

Religious affiliation Christian-based, but open to all

Services provided Parent support; curriculum; curriculum resources; networking; homeschooling information; annual convention; newsletter

L.E.A.R.N.
3703 Merrimac Trail
Annandale, VA 22003
Phone: (703) 560-5108
E-mail: JntteSmith@aol.com
Contact person: Jeannette Smith (Contact person changes every one
                                  or two years)

Area of influence Regional (Northern Virginia, D.C., Maryland)

Religious affiliation Nonsectarian

Services provided Curriculum resources: other educational resources; networking (homeschooling families and other agencies); annual convention (through HEAV); newsletter; field trips; clubs; discussion groups; workshops

Statement "L.E.A.R.N. is an inclusive network providing homeschool-related information and support to homeschoolers and prospective homeschoolers." Monthly newsletter includes children's contributions.

Virginia Home Education Association
P.O. Box 5131
Charlottesville, VA 22905
Phone: (540) 832-3578
E-mail: vhea@virginia.edu

Web site: http://poe.acc.virginia.edu/~pm6f/vhea.html
Contact person: Will Shaw, President (Contact person changes every
       two years)

Area of influence   Statewide

Religious affiliation   None

Services provided   Referral; networking (other agencies); legislation
monitoring; homeschooling information; newsletter; speakers

Statement   The purpose of the VHEA is to "promote, defend, and ex-
plain home education; provide information to and communicate with
homeschooling individuals, families, and groups; maintain relations with
public education interests; represent homeschool interests to government
and public education officials, legislators, the media and the public."
Web site contains links to other sites, including many in Virginia.

Virginia Department of Education
James Monroe Building
101 N. Fourteenth Street
P.O. Box 2120
Richmond, VA 23218-2120
Phone: (804) 225-2020 (General information)

WASHINGTON

Family Learning Organization
P.O. Box 7247
Spokane, WA 99207-0247
Phone: (509) 924-3760
       (509) 467-2552
Fax: 1-800-405-8378 (Call to arrange fax)
E-mail: kathleenflo@bluezebra.com
Web site: coming soon
Contact person: Kathleen McCurdy

Area of influence   Statewide; National testing

Religious affiliation   None

Services provided   Parent support; referral; networking (homeschooling families and other agencies); legislation monitoring; homeschool-

ing information; newsletter: *The Current;* testing services (standardized tests); how-to-homeschool classes and workshops

Statement Family Learning Organization believes "that we are to serve families interested in home education to the best of our ability regardless of race, creed, methods used, or reasons for homeschooling. Recognizing that families represent varied and unique perspectives on education, whether structured or unstructured, religious or secular, we believe that having choices and options is the best way to ensure more freedom for all. In keeping with our purpose, we support measures that promote parental involvement in education in all instances, even in the schools."

Homeschoolers' Support Association
P.O. Box 413
Maple Valley, WA 98038
Phone: (425) 746-5047
Contact person: Teresa Sparling (Contact person changes every two
               or three years)

Area of influence Regional

Religious affiliation Nonsectarian

Services provided Parent support; referral; networking (homeschooling and other agencies); homeschooling information; newsletter; children's activities, including field trips and get-togethers

Statement "HSA is a large local homeschooling support group serving over 500 families in the South Puget Sound area. We offer information and support to homeschooling families and those considering the homeschooling option."

Inland Empire Home School Center
P.O. Box 1750
Airway Heights, WA 99001
Phone: (509) 299-3766
Fax: (509) 299-3766
E-mail: hammer@cet.com/MTS22@juno.com
Web site: pending

Area of influence Regional (Washington and surrounding states)

Religious affiliation Nonsectarian

Services provided Parent support; referral; curriculum resources; other educational resources; legislation monitoring; homeschooling information; newsletter: *Inland Empire Home School News;* testing and evaluation of students' progress

Statement "Since 1985, the Inland Empire Home School Center has operated a full-service resource center for homeschool families in the greater Northwest. We have many different resources available through our extensive database referral network. Our primary focus for the last six years has been testing and evaluation of student progress through our Academic Skills Assessment Program, a comprehensive diagnostic tool for students age 8 to 18."

Network of Vancouver Area Homeschoolers (NOVAH)
162 Krogstad Road
Washougal, WA 98671
Phone: (360) 837-3760
Fax: (360) 837-3733
E-mail: 71230.66@compuserve.com
Contact person: Lori Loranger

Area of influence Regional (three counties)

Religious affiliation None

Services provided Parent support; curriculum resources; other educational resources; networking (homeschooling families); homeschooling information; newsletter

Statement "NOVAH welcomes members without regard to race, religion, politics, or personal lifestyle. NOVAH is a voluntary association for homeschooling support, and operates without fees or dues. We have regular informal gatherings for parents and children, and maintain a network of information sharing."

Washington Homeschool Organization
18130 Midvale Avenue N, Suite C
Shoreline, WA 98133
Phone: (206) 546-9483
Fax: (206) 546-1810

E-mail: WHOoffice@juno.com
Web site: http://www.washhomeschool.org
Contact person: Sherry, office secretary (Contact person changes
　　　　　　　　periodically)

Area of influence　Statewide

Religious affiliation　None

Services provided　Parent support; referral curriculum resources; other
educational resources; networking (homeschooling families and other
agencies); annual convention; newsletter: *WHO's News;* student expo;
high school graduation ceremony; maintains list of support groups in
Washington State

Statement　"WHO is a statewide organization dedicated to serving the
homeschoolers in Washington State. We are a support and information
network serving the diverse and multifaceted interests of home-based
education. Our purpose is to assist parents who are considering homeschooling to make an informed choice and to offer resource information
and support to those who have chosen the homeschooling option."

Whatcom Homeschool Association
3851 Britton Road
Bellingham, WA 98226
Phone: (360) 671-3689
Fax: (360) 647-6052
E-mail: garym@dis-corp.com
Contact persons: Gary and Bobbe McGill

Area of influence　Regional

Religious affiliation　None

Services provided　Parent support; curriculum; referral; curriculum
resources; other educational resources; networking (homeschooling
families and fifty other agencies); legislation monitoring; homeschooling information; annual convention; newsletter: *WHA's Happening;*
organized field trips and activities; workshops; lending library; annual
open house to exhibit children's work; standardized testing service

Statement　WHA, which started in 1984, "is a group of Whatcom
County families who want to work together to make homeschooling
an enjoyable learning experience."

Public Instruction Department
P.O. Box 47200 (Old Capitol Building)
Olympia, WA 98504-7200
Phone: (360) 753-6738 (General information)

WEST VIRGINIA

West Virginia Department of Education
1900 Kanawha Boulevard, East
Charleston, WV 25305
Phone: (304) 558-2440

WISCONSIN

Wisconsin Christian Home Educators Association
2307 Carmel Avenue
Racine, WI 53405
Phone: (414) 637-5127
Fax: (414) 638-8127
E-mail: jang@execpc.com
Contact person: Jan Gnacinski

Area of influence   Statewide

Religious affiliation   Christian

Services provided   Parent support; curriculum resources; other educational resources; networking (homeschooling families); legislation monitoring; homeschooling information; two annual conventions; newsletter; information packet on homeschooling

Wisconsin Parents Association
P.O. Box 2502
Madison, WI 53701-2502
Phone: (608) 283-3131 (Voice mail)
Phone: (608) 283-3131 (orders)
Web site: http://www.alumni.caltech.edu/~casner/wpa/

Area of influence   Statewide

Religious affiliation   None

Services/materials provided Parent support; homeschooling information/ publications; annual conference, curriculum fair and used book sale; newsletter; legislation information; handbook; information reprints; legislative alerts; WPA/homeschooling packet of information distributed to public libraries

Statement "Wisconsin Parents Association is a statewide grassroots organization of 1,000 families that has been serving homeschoolers in Wisconsin since 1984. WPA provides speakers on homeschooling for library programs, public information meetings, and local homeschooling support group meetings." The WPA handbook, *Homeschooling in Wisconsin: At Home With Learning,* provides encouragement and support, practical information, and easily accessible legal information for homeschooling families.

State of Wisconsin Department of Public Instruction
P.O. Box 7841
Madison, WI 53707-7841
Phone: (608) 266-3390 (General information)

WYOMING

Homeschoolers of Wyoming
P.O. Box 907
Evansville, WY 82636
Phone: (307) 237-4383
Fax: (307) 237-3080
Contact person: Mary Sunderman (Contact person changes every two
                 years; will change in June 1999)

Area of influence Statewide

Religious affiliation Multi-denominational Christian

Services provided Parent support; referral; curriculum resources; legislation monitoring; homeschooling information; annual convention

Statement "The purpose of H.O.W. is to provide support for Wyoming families which home educate. H.O.W. is a statewide group led by seven district officers who are Christians. These seven state officials advise and inform the twenty county contacts throughout the state who work with their local support groups to provide information and put together activities."

Wyoming State Department of Education
Hathaway Building, 2nd Floor
2300 Capitol Avenue
Cheyenne, WY 82002-0050
Phone: (307) 777-6206 (General information)

Canada

ALBERTA

Alberta Department of Education
Private School Coordinator
West Tower, Devonian Bldg.
11160 Jasper Avenue
Edmonton, Alberta T5K 0L2 Canada
Phone: (403) 427-7219
Fax: (403) 427-0591

BRITISH COLUMBIA

Canadian Home Educators' Association of British Columbia
6980 Marble Hill Road
Chilliwack, British Columbia V2P 6H3 Canada
Phone: (250) 493-0338
Fax: (604) 794-3940
E-mail: cheabc@imag.net
Web site: http://www.flora.org/homeschool-ca/bc/chea.htm
Contact person: Colleen Erzinger, President (Contact person changes
                every two years)

Area of influence   Provincial

Religious affiliation   None

Services provided   Parent support; referral; curriculum resources; other educational resources; networking (homeschooling families and other agencies); legislation monitoring; homeschooling information; annual convention; newsletter: *CHEA News;* public relations; research; legal defense

Statement   "CHEA is a registered nonprofit society dedicated to the protection of the family's freedom to educate children at home. It was formed in 1988 as an umbrella organization to represent all home schoolers regardless of their philosophical or religious beliefs. CHEA has the recognition from the Ministry of Education as an organization through which the Ministry can communicate with home educators."

British Columbia Ministry of Education
Independent Schools Branch
Parliament Buildings
Victoria, British Columbia V8V 2M4 Canada
Phone: (604) 356-0432
Fax: (604) 387-9695

MANITOBA

Manitoba Homeschool Resource Page
Web site: http://www.flora.org/homeschool-ca/test/

Includes rules and regulations for Manitoba homeschoolers; sample educational plan; progress reports, etc.

Manitoba Department of Education
Home School Coordinator
555 Main Street
Winkler, Manitoba R6W 1C4 Canada
Phone: (204) 325-2309
        1-800-465-9915
Fax: (204) 325-4212

NEW BRUNSWICK

New Brunswick Department of Education
P.O. Box 6000
Fredericton, New Brunswick E3B 5H1 Canada
Phone: (506) 453-3678
Fax: (506) 453-3325

NEWFOUNDLAND

Newfoundland Department of Education and Training
Government of Newfoundland and Labrador
Confederation Building, West Block
Box 8700
St. John's, Newfoundland A1B 4J6 Canada
Phone: (709) 729-5097
Fax: (709) 729-5896

NORTHWEST TERRITORIES

Northwest Territories Department of Education, Culture &
Employment
Educational Development
P.O. Box 1320
Yellowknife, Northwest Territories X1A 2L9 Canada
Phone: (403) 920-8061
Fax: (403) 873-0155

NOVA SCOTIA

Nova Scotia Home Education Association
c/o Marion Homer
RR #1
Rose Bay, Nova Scotia B0J 2X0 Canada
Phone: (902) 766-4355
E-mail: marion.f.homer@ns.sympatico.ca
Web site: http://www.glinx.com/users/dietert/nshea.htm
Contact person: Marion Homer

Area of influence   Provincial

Religious affiliation   None

Services provided   Referral; networking (homeschooling families and
other agencies); legislation monitoring; homeschooling information;
annual curriculum fair; newsletter; serves as liaison to the Nova Scotia Department of Education; sets up field trips

Statement   "The purpose of the organization is to promote the awareness of home schooling within the province, to safeguard the rights of
home schooling families, and to represent their interests at provincial
and local levels."

Nova Scotia Department of Education
Box 578
Halifax, Nova Scotia B3J 2S9 Canada
Phone: (902) 424-5829
Fax: (902) 424-0519

ONTARIO

Natural Life (formerly Canadian Alliance of Homeschoolers)
RR 1
St. George, Ontario N0E 1N0 Canada
Fax: (519) 448-4411
Web site: http://www.life.ca
Contact person: Wendy Priesnitz

Statement "Natural Life has become a trusted source of information on deschooling and maintains links with thousands of home-based educators around the world." They also offer a mentor/apprentice exchange. Web site contains informative articles on various aspects of homeschooling, as well as an up-to-date annotated directory of local Canadian homeschooling groups arranged by province.

Ontario Federation of Teaching Parents
145 Taylor Road, W, RR #1
Gananoque, Ontario K7G 2U3 Canada
Phone: (613) 382-4947
E-mail: heyj@adan.kingston.net
Web site: http://www.flora.org/oftp
Contact person: Herb Jones (Contact person changes every three years)

Area of influence Provincial

Religious affiliation None

Services provided Parent support; curriculum resources; other educational resources; legislation monitoring; homeschooling information; annual convention; newsletter

Statement The purpose of the organization is "to dispense information and resources on and for home education and educators, with the goal of bridging the gap between families and school boards/Ministry of Education on legal issues and resolving concerns."

Ontario Ministry of Education & Training
Provincial School Attendance Counselor
Tenth Floor, Mowat Block
900 Bay Street
Toronto, Ontario M7A 1L2 Canada
Phone: (416) 325-2224
Fax: (416) 325-2552

PRINCE EDWARD ISLAND

Prince Edward Island Department of Education
Box 2000
Charlottetown, Prince Edward Island C1A 7N8 Canada
Phone: (902) 368-4600
Fax: (902) 368-4663

QUEBEC

Quebec Minnistere de l'Education
1035 Rue De La Chevrotiere
Quebec, Quebec G1R 5A5 Canada
Phone: (418) 643-7095
Fax: (418) 646-6561

SASKATCHEWAN

Saskatchewan Home-Based Educators
Suite 13, 403 – 22nd Street West
Saskatoon, Saskatchewan S7M 5T3 Canada
Phone: (306) 545-3532
      1-888-233-7423 (toll-free in Saskatchewan only)
E-mail: alramsey@dlcwest.com
Web site: http://www.dlcwest.com/~shbe/
Contact person: Al Ramsey (Contact person changes every several years)

Area of influence Provincial (local support groups)

Religious affiliation Nonsectarian

Services provided Parent support; networking (homeschooling families); legislation monitoring; homeschooling information; annual conference; newsletter; social and educational networking; regional information meetings and seminars

Statement "Saskatchewan Home-Based Educators is the official voice of home-based educators in Saskatchewan. We assist in creating a positive social network and a positive political environment for those who choose home-based education. Additionally we provide supportive, social, and instructional resources to our membership."

Saskatchewan Department of Education, Training & Employment
Independent Schools & Home-Based Education
3085 Albert Street
Regina, Saskatchewan S4P 3V7 Canada
Phone: (306) 787-7054
Fax: (306) 787-6139

YUKON

Yukon Territory Department of Education
Government of the Yukon Territory
P.O. Box 2703
Whitehorse, Yukon Territory Y1A 2C6 Canada
Phone: (403) 667-5607
Fax: (403) 667-6339

For more information regarding Canadian provincial homeschool support groups and regulations, see:

Canadian Homeschooling Resource Page
http://www.flora.org/homeschool-ca/

This Web site has: a page for each province; a Homeschool Chat Room; Canadian Homeschool Mail List (a place for general homeschool discussions); listings of homeschooling conferences; Canadian books, catalogs and resources; Canadian homeschool news; education-related sites; Homeschool Keypals; FAQs; Canadian universities accepting homeschoolers; and links to many homeschool-related pages and to Education Department sites for the provinces.

Correspondence Schools

Bob Jones University Press
Greenville, SC 29614
Phone: (864) 242-5100 (orders)
          1-800-845-5731
Fax: (864) 298-0268
E-mail: bjup@bju.edu
Web site: http://www.bju.edu/press

Distribution area   National

Religious affiliation   Nondenominational Protestant

Age levels served   Preschool–18 years (PreS–grade 12)

Materials/services provided   Parent support; curriculum materials; educational enrichment materials; homeschooling information/publications; testing and evaluation service (nationally standardized tests; diploma for high school graduates; newsletter: *Home School Helper* (4 issues/year)

Statement   Additional special services offered include: the Academy of Home Education—a high school home education program, which includes test administration, transcript and diploma; BJ LINC—a live interactive network classroom; HOMESAT—delayed broadcast of BJ LINC to the home VCR for later viewing by homeschoolers. Bob Jones University also hosts an annual Home Educators Leadership

Program the first week in June—a weeklong homeschool conference featuring prominent speakers and over 150 workshops.

Boston School
P.O. Box 2920
Big Bear City, CA 92314
Phone: (909) 585-7188
Web site: http://www.Bostonschool.org
Contact person: Susan Jordan, Director

Distribution area   National

Religious affiliation   None

Age levels served   5–18 years (K–grade 12)

Materials/services provided   Parent support; homeschooling information/ publications; legislation information; testing; referral; diploma for high school graduates; newsletter (4 issues/year)

Type of curriculum   "Parents choose their own materials. We serve families who use preset curriculum and families with an unschooling philosophy. We individualize each student's program." Newsletter keeps members informed on education issues, politics, and theories.

Statement   "Boston School is an inclusive organization. We believe each child develops at an individual pace and curriculum needs to be adjusted to the individual. Each family has its own values that need to be respected. The family, child, and school work together to put together an educational package that meets the needs of both the child and family."

Calvert School
105 Tuscany Road
Baltimore, MD 21210
Phone: (410) 243-6030
Fax: (401) 366-0674
Web site: http://www.calvertschool.org
Contact person: Susan Weiss, Principal, Home Instruction Department

Distribution area   National

Religious affiliation   None

Age levels served   K–grade 8

Materials/services provided   Complete curriculum; textbooks; testing; academic counseling

Type of curriculum   "Calvert's home instruction courses are drawn from the outstanding Calvert Day School curriculum. The essence of a Calvert education is a solid grounding in the basics. Traditional methodologies are used to inculcate strong skills and to teach an important body of knowledge. Together these skills and this knowledge will serve the student well in future endeavors."

Statement   "Calvert school, established in 1899, is incorporated as a nonprofit organization and is internationally recognized among independent schools. Its courses are approved by the Maryland State Department of Education. The school is a member of the Educational Records Bureau and the National Association of Independent Schools."

Clonlara School
1289 Jewett
Ann Arbor, MI 48104
Phone: (313) 769-4511
Fax: (313) 769-9629
E-mail: clonlara@delphi.com
Web site: http://www.clonlara.org
Contact person: Terri Wheeler

Distribution area   National

Religious affiliation   None

Age levels served   5–18 years (K–grade 12)

Materials/services provided   Complete curriculum; parent support; homeschooling information/publications; legislation information; testing; academic counseling; diploma for high school graduates; newsletter (6 issues/year)

Type of curriculum   Individualized curriculum—"a living document which can be tailored to fit the academic needs of the student." Purpose of newsletter is: "to educate and update our homeschooling families with newsworthy information." Newsletter contains resources, announcements, featured articles from the director, regional news, support corner, student writings. Non-enrolled families can subscribe to the newsletter for $15/year.

Statement "Clonlara School is a fully functioning private day school with an extension program to assist home educators. It aims to 'create an environment where children and parents are free to guide their own learning. Close team efforts with student and parent are encouraged and developed.'"

Eagle Academy
49 Violet Avenue
Poughkeepsie, NY 12601-1520
Phone: (914) 454-5324
E-mail: eagle@mhv.net
Web site: http://www.eagle.mhv.net
Contact person: Jean De Fino, Director of Administration

Distribution area   National

Religious affiliation   None

Materials/services provided   Complete curriculum; testing; academic counseling; transcripts; suggestions for materials

Type of curriculum   Eagle Academy offers three educational services: Basic, Enrolled, and Mentored.

Statement "Eagle Academy is an information age learning center established in cyberspace with the vision of harnessing the tools of our technological age for the purpose of educating the next generation. The focus is on the support of parents who choose to utilize home schooling as the method of education for their children."

Home Study International
12501 Old Columbia Pike
Silver Spring, MD 20294-6600
Phone: (301) 680-6570 (information)
         1-800-782-4769

Fax: (301) 680-6577
E-mail: 74617.74@compuserve.com
Contact person: Kathleen Sowards

Distribution area National

Religious affiliation Seventh-day Adventist

Age levels served Preschool–18 years (PreS–grade 12)

Materials/services provided Complete curriculum; specialized curriculum; textbooks; homeschooling information/publications; testing; academic counseling; diploma for high school graduates; newsletter (4 issues/year) for members

Type of curriculum "HSI is a Christian home school curriculum provider. You may choose to buy books only, all supplies including parent's guides with daily lesson plans, or opt for the full package that includes accreditation, teacher services, transcripts, etc. Tuition and supply costs vary depending on grade and courses."

Statement "As a global Seventh-day Adventist educational institution, the mission of Home Study International is to provide educationally sound, values-based, guided independent study and distance education programs that build a foundation for service to God, church, and society. The programs and courses, which respond to learner needs in the context of a lifetime learning experience, are available to all who can benefit from them."

Laurel Springs School
1002 E. Ojai Avenue *or*
P.O. Box 1440
Ojai, CA 93024
Phone: (805) 646-2473
Fax: (805) 646-0186
E-mail: lss@laurelsprings.com
Web site: http://www.laurelsprings.com
Contact person: Marilyn Mosley

Distribution area National

Religious affiliation None

Age levels served   Preschool–18 years (PreS–grade 12)

Materials/services provided   Complete curriculum; specialized curriculum; textbooks; curriculum enrichment materials; parent support; testing; academic counseling; diploma for high school graduates; newsletter (10 issues/year)

Type of curriculum   "We offer standard textbook curriculum as well as online curriculum, which we adjust to meet the needs of individual students."

Statement   "Laurel Springs' philosophy is that children learn best when they are motivated and excited by learning. We try to find the child's area of interest and expand it. The result is a child who performs well and gains self-confidence." Newsletter keeps families informed of Laurel Springs activities.

Oak Meadow School
P.O. Box 740
Putney, VT 05346
Phone: (802) 387-2021
Fax: (802) 387-5108
E-mail: 75331.1743@compuserve.com
Web site: http://www.oakmeadow.com/
Contact persons: Bonnie Williams, Administrative Director
                Dr. Lawrence T. Williams, Educational Director

Distribution area   National

Religious affiliation   None

Age levels served   5–18 (K–grade 12)

Materials/services provided   Complete curriculum; specialized curriculum; parent/teacher and creative parenting home study courses; textbooks; parent support; homeschooling information/publications; testing; academic counseling; diploma for high school graduates; newsletter: *Living Education* (6 issues/year); *Learning Dynamics* audiocassettes to help understand the learning process

Type of curriculum   "The Oak Meadow curriculum is written to accommodate a wide variety of learning styles and provide opportunities for all children to learn easily, effectively, and enjoyably." Oak Meadow offers four options for learning: 1. enrollment with a curriculum and teacher support; 2. enrollment with an Individualized Educational Program (IEP), "created to meet the unique interests and abilities of individual students"; 3. enrollment with a Portfolio Evaluation (parents responsible for student support, testing, and portfolio of completed work and student evaluation—Oak Meadow teacher evaluates student's work and completes grade report); 4. Oak Meadow curriculum without enrollment.

Statement   "Since 1975, Oak Meadow has been creating integrative learning programs for parents and children around the world, based upon four proven principles of learning—Involve the whole child. Cooperate with the natural cycles of unfoldment. Create a caring relationship. Adapt to each child's learning style. Courses and programs are developed by experienced homeschooling teachers who know how to create effective learning environments. In addition to providing a firm foundation for academic excellence, Oak Meadow courses show you how to cooperate with individual learning styles and natural unfoldment processes to maximize your child's potential for imaginative activity and creative thought." OnLine Directory allows networking with Oak Meadow families around the world.

Pearblossom Private School, Inc.
P.O. Box 847
Pearblossom, CA 93553
Phone: (805) 944-0914 (information)
        1-800-309-3569 (orders)
Fax: (805) 944-4483
Contact person: Rusty L. Goldman

Distribution area   National

Religious affiliation   None

Age levels served   5–18 (K–grade 12)

Materials/services provided   Complete curriculum; specialized curriculum; textbooks; curriculum enrichment materials; parent support; homeschooling information/publications; testing; academic counseling; diploma for high school graduates; newsletter (6 issues/year); R-FORCE (Remote Consulting Education: one-on-one contact for student questions and assistance)

Type of curriculum "The Elementary School Curriculum provides an integrated approach to learning, with each lesson building on the previous one. For high school we provide outstanding textbooks for each subject. The student completes standardized and out-of-chapter texts that are graded by the school."

Santa Fe Community School
P.O. Box 2241
Santa Fe, NM 87504-2241
Phone: (505) 471-6928
Fax: (505) 474-3220
Contact persons: Mary Warner, Secretary
 Ed Nagel, Principal

Distribution area National

Religious affiliation None

Age levels served 5–18 (K–grade 12)

Materials/services provided Referral; other educational resources; networking (other agencies); homeschooling information; student records; diploma for high school graduates; newsletter: *Home Study Exchange* (5 issues/year)

Type of curriculum "We provide help, if necessary, to the parents and students in designing and implementing their own home study curriculum, based on the student's interests."

Statement "Santa Fe Community School is a private school, based on the philosophy of Summerhill, that offers a Home Study program for students across the country and around the world. We are non-coercive, ungraded, and non-graded. We do not believe in testing, but we do believe in being open, honest, and real with everyone (including children), and in allowing children to make their own decisions, giving guidance when necessary."

Silver Crest School
Family Learning Services, Inc.
P.O. Box 9
Junction City, OR 97448-0009
Phone: (541) 998-5735

Fax: (541) 998-5737
E-mail: crymes@rio.com
Web site: http://www.fls-homeschool.com
Contact person: Suzanne Crymes, Administrator

Distribution area National

Religious affiliation Nonsectarian Christian, but families of all ethnic origins and religions are welcome

Age levels served Preschool–18 (PreS–grade 12)

Materials/services provided Complete curriculum; specialized curriculum; textbooks; curriculum enrichment materials; legal information; parent support; testing; academic counseling; career counseling; diploma for high school graduates; individual staff support; maintenance of student file records; newsletter: *The Pointer;* independent study; career/life transition counseling

Type of curriculum "Family Learning Services, in cooperation with families, will assist in designing alternative educational programs to facilitate meeting the needs of each student. Students who are enrolled in Silver Crest School, an academic program administered by Family Learning Services, receive the benefits of quality supervision and curriculum suggestions that can be tailored to fit personal learning styles and abilities. These supportive services provide study options under an umbrella program providing an individual education plan that will guide students in fulfilling requirements for each grade level. High school students can broaden their learning experiences further by doing volunteer work or an internship."

Statement "One of the most important aspects of education is providing structure and guidance for the learner. The ultimate goal is not only to assist in the education of students, but to assist families as they provide an atmosphere conducive to academic learning, spiritual growth, social development, and physical fitness." Administration of Structure of Intellect (SOI) tests, internationally recognized assessment tools, is offered by Family Learning Services to students of various ages. These tests help to identify each individual's unique profile of learning strengths and weaknesses, and can lead to an individual training program that will help the student to improve study skills, concentration, creativity, and more.

The Sycamore Tree Center for Home Education
2179 Meyer Place
Costa Mesa, CA 92627
Phone: (714) 650-4466 (information)
      1-800-779-6750 (orders)
Fax: (714) 642-6750
E-mail: sycamoretree@compuserve.com
Web site: http://www.sycamoretree.com
Contact person: Sandy Gogel

Distribution area   National/International

Religious affiliation   Nonsectarian Christian

Age levels served   Preschool–18 (PreS–grade 12)

Materials/services provided   Complete curriculum; specialized curriculum; textbooks; curriculum enrichment materials; parent support; homeschooling information/publications; testing; academic counseling; diploma for high school graduates; newsletter (10 issues/year); individualized study program

Type of curriculum   "We offer a complete homeschool program for K–12. In addition, we have a mail order catalog of over 3,000 curricular and supplemental materials."

Statement   In addition to the services listed above, The Sycamore Tree Educational Services offers "professional educational guidance by phone or mail, support groups in each area where Sycamore Tree families are located, 70- to 80-page packet of educational enrichment material each month with parent helps, and more. We are currently planning an online school beginning in September 1998."

Upattinas School and Resource Center
429 Greenridge Road
Glenmoore, PA 19343
Phone: (610) 458-5138
Fax: (610) 458-8688
E-mail: upatinas@chesco.com
Web site: http://www.chesco.com/upattinas
Contact person: Sandra M. Hurst

Distribution area　National

Religious affiliation　None

Age levels served　5–18 (K–grade 12)

Materials/services provided　Complete curriculum; specialized curriculum; textbooks; curriculum enrichment materials; parent support; homeschooling information/publications; legislation information; testing; academic counseling; referral; diploma for high school graduates; newsletter (5 issues/year)

Type of curriculum　"Our program is very informal and child-centered, and completely optional. We can be formal if needed."

Statement　"Home study with Upattinas Resource Center is individualized according to the needs of each family. Our underlying philosophy of non-coercive and democratic learning leads us to encourage people to allow time for play and experiential learning at all ages and not to worry about grade levels. Upattinas encourages families to create their own curriculum plans and to be flexible with those plans so that opportunities or interests that arise unexpectedly can be explored at any time. We neither require nor recommend a structured daily plan or prescribed textbooks and workbooks for our students. We have developed yearly plans for each grade level (for those families who feel the need for a plan to guide them)." Classes and part-time programs are available on campus, as well.

Publishers and Distributors of Homeschooling Resources

A Beka Book
P.O. Box 18000
Pensacola, FL 32523-9160
Phone: 1-800-874-2352 (U.S. & Canada) 8:00–4:30 Central time
1-800-874-7472 (24-hour orders)
Fax: 1-800-874-3590

Distribution area National

Religious affiliation Christian—national publishing arm of Pensacola Christian College, a training school for Christian educators

Age levels served Preschool–18 (PreK–grade 12)

Materials provided Curriculum materials (all subjects); video correspondence programs

Subject specialty Full curriculum

Academic Distribution Services (ADS)
528 Carnarvon Street
New Westminster, British Columbia V3L 1C4 Canada
Phone: (604) 524-9758 (information)
1-800-276-0078 (orders)
E-mail: ads@intergate.bc.ca
Web site: ads@ads-academic.com

Distribution area   Canada (National)

Religious affiliation   None

Age levels served   13–18

Materials provided   Parent support; curriculum materials; educational enrichment materials (games, software, flashcards, etc.)

Subject specialty   Canadian social studies; French

AIMS Education Foundation
P.O. Box 8120
Fresno, CA 93747-8120
Phone: (209) 255-4094 (information)
    (888) 733-2467 (orders)
Fax: (209) 255-6396
E-mail: aimsed@fresno.edu
Web site: http://www.aimsedu.org

Distribution area   National

Religious affiliation   None

Age levels served   5–14 (K–grade 9)

Materials provided   Curriculum materials; educational enrichment materials (games, kits, science and laboratory items, etc.); homeschooling information/publications; basic information packet; *AIMS Magazine* (10 issues/year)—includes classroom activities/investigations, math and science, puzzles, problem solving activities, discrepant events, dialogues, and building instructional aids

Subject specialty   Math, science, technology (Note: AIMS is the acronym for Activities Integrating Mathematics and Science.)

Statement   "AIMS has earned a national reputation for its leadership in developing an integrated science/mathematics/technology curriculum and building a quality staff-development program to support its successful implementation."

Ampersand Press
750 Lake Street
Port Townsend, WA 98368
Phone: (360) 379-5187
    1-800-624-4263
Fax: (360) 379-0324
E-mail: mooburg@olympus.net
Web site: http://www.ampersandpress.com

Distribution area   National

Religious affiliation   None

Age levels served   Preschool–19 (K–grade 12)

Materials provided   Educational enrichment materials (games, rubber stamps)

Subject specialty   Nature and science themes

Statement   Ampersand Press is a game and rubber stamp manufacturer committed to promoting environmental awareness through interactive fun.

Blue Bird Publishing
2266 S. Dobson, #275
Mesa, AZ 85202
Phone: (602) 831-6063
    1-888-672-2275 (toll-free ordering)
Fax: (602) 831-1829
E-mail: bluebird@bluebird1.com
Web site: http://www.bluebird1.com

Distribution area   National

Religious affiliation   None

Materials provided/Subject specialty   Books for parents and teachers on homeschooling, parenting, and education; also, Cheryl Gorder will design, publish, market, and distribute books for other authors

Bluestocking Press
P.O. Box 2030–S
Shingle Springs, CA 95682-2030
Phone: (916) 621-1123 (information)
        1-800-959-8586 (orders)
Fax: (916) 642-9222

Distribution area   National

Religious affiliation   None

Age levels served   Preschool–18 (K–grade 12)

Materials provided   Catalog (K–12) niched to American history and excellent higher-level math program for ages 12 and up; *Home School Market Guide*—a special marketing report on the homeschooling market for businesses who are trying to access this market. This publication includes a master directory of conferences, reviewers, mail lists, advertising opportunities, and more.

Subject specialty   American history, economics, and law; publisher of the "Uncle Eric" books by Richard J. Maybury; also specializes in books by and about Laura Ingalls Wilder

Boston School Bookstore
P.O. Box 1827
Big Bear Lake, CA 92315
Phone (909) 584-9540
Fax: (909) 584-9540
E-mail: bookstore@bigbear.net
Contact person: David Zimmerman

Distribution area   National

Religious affiliation   None

Age levels served   Preschool–18 (PreS–grade 12)

Materials provided   Complete curriculum; specialized curriculum; textbooks; curriculum enrichment materials (games; educational computer software; computer hardware)

Canadian Home Education Resources
7 Stanley Cr.
Calgary, Alberta, T2S 1G1 Canada
Phone: (403) 243-9727
Fax: (403) 243-9727
E-mail: cher@cadvision.com

Distribution area   Canada (National)

Religious affiliation   Christian

Age levels served   Preschool–18 (PreS–grade 12)

Materials provided   Parent support; curriculum materials; textbooks; educational enrichment materials (games covering all subject areas, etc.); mail order catalog

Common Sense Press
P.O. Box 1365
Melrose, FL 32666
Phone: (954) 962-1930 (information)
          (352) 475-5757 (orders)
Fax: (352) 475-6105
E-mail: learnCSP@aol.com

Distribution area   International

Religious affiliation   Christian oriented

Age levels served   Preschool–18 (PreS–grade 12)

Materials provided   Curriculum materials; educational enrichment materials

Subject specialty   Homeschool curriculum for purchase by dealers

Creative Teaching Press, Inc./Youngheart Music
10701 Holder Street
Cypress, CA 90630
Phone: 1-800-444-4287 (information and orders)
Fax: 1-800-229-9929
E-mail: welisten@creativeteaching.com

Web site: creativeteaching.com
Contact person: Tania Pickrell, Marketing Specialist

Distribution area   National

Religious affiliation   None

Age levels served   Preschool–18 (PreS–grade 12)

Materials provided   Curriculum materials; educational enrichment materials (classroom decoratives, floor puzzles, and more); home-schooling information/publications; musical audio and video products (children's, family, and educational)

Statement   The mission of Creative Teaching Press is "enriching the lives of children, teachers, and parents by developing creative, exciting quality educational products."

Cuisenaire/Dale Seymour Publications
125 Greenbush Road South
Orangeburg, NY 10962
Phone: 1-800-237-0388 or 1-800-872-1100 (24 hours)
        1-800-237-3142 (Customer service)
Fax: 1-800-RODS
E-mail: info@awl.com
Web site: http://www.cuisenaire.com
        http://www.awl.com/dsp/

Distribution area   National

Religious affiliation   None

Age levels served   5–18 (K–grade 12)

Materials provided   Curriculum materials; educational enrichment materials (including math manipulatives); activity-based mathematics curriculums funded by the National Science Foundation

Subject specialty   Math, science

Statement   Cuisenaire/Dale Seymour Publications is a division of Addison Wesley Longman Supplementary Group, jointly representing more than 75 years of educational expertise. "Our shared commitment is to provide K–12 educators with high-quality educational resources for math, science, and the arts, emphasizing hands-on learning and problem-solving and higher order thinking skills."

Curriculum Associates
153 Rangeway Road
P.O. Box 2001
North Billerica, MA 01862-0901
Phone: 1-800-225-0248 (information and orders)
Fax: 1-800-366-1158
E-mail: sales@cahomeschool.com
Web site: http://www.cahomeschool.com

Distribution area   National

Religious affiliation   None

Age levels served   Preschool–18 (PreS–grade 12)

Materials provided   Curriculum materials (various subjects); high school proficiency test preparation; other test preparations; teacher resources; math software; Jackie Torrence storytelling videos

The Education Connection
Phone: 1-800-887-6891 (24 hours)
Fax: (970) 493-5409
E-mail: carlile@edconnect.com
Web site: http://www.edconnect.com/whyteci.htm

Distribution area   National

Religious affiliation   None

Materials provided   Learning enhancement tools, such as 3-D puzzles, maps and mapping kit, telescopes, aircraft activity and model kit, kits for exploring ancient cultures and the five senses, storytime card kits (story starters), puppet playhouse

Statement   "We are committed to helping children connect with science, nature, and art. We accomplish this by offering gifts that educate, stimulate, and entertain young minds."

The Elijah Company
1053 Eldridge Loop
Crossville, TN 38555
Phone: (615) 456-6284 (information)
      1-888-2ELIJAH (orders)
Fax: (615) 456-6384
Web site: http://www.elijahco.com

Distribution area   National

Religious affiliation   Christian

Age levels served   Preschool–18 (K–grade 12)

Materials provided   Parent support; curriculum materials; educational enrichment materials; 200-page catalog

Subject specialty   Homeschooling materials

Family Learning Services
P.O. Box 9596
Birmingham, AL 35220
Phone: (205) 854-6870 (information and orders)
Fax: (205) 520-1143
E-mail: Awardsales@aol.com

Distribution area   National

Religious affiliation   Christian

Age levels served   Preschool–18 (PreS–grade 12)

Materials provided   Parent support; curriculum materials; educational enrichment materials (games, software, etc.); homeschooling information/ publications; catalog of publications

FUN Books (Family Unschoolers Network)
1688 Belhaven Woods Ct.
Pasadena, MD 21122-3727
Voice mail/Fax: (410) 360-7330
E-mail: FUNNews@MCImail.com
Web site: http://members.aol.com/FUNNews

Distribution area   National

Religious affiliation   None

Materials provided   Curriculum materials; curriculum enrichment (books, games, toys, coloring books, Cuisenaire rods, craft books; paper dolls); homeschooling information/publications; parenting books; catalog lists some homeschooling Web sites

Genius Tribe
P.O. Box 1014
Eugene, OR 97440
Phone: (541) 686-2315 (information and orders)
Fax: (541) 343-3158
E-mail: GraceJanet@aol.com
Web site: http://home.aol.com/GTcatalog

Distribution area   National/International

Religious affiliation   None

Age levels served   All, but especially 13–18 (grades 7–12)

Materials provided   Curriculum materials (many subjects); books on homeschooling and parenting; educational enrichment materials; summer camp for homeschooling teenagers

Subject specialty   Unschooling/learner-directed education

Statement   Genius Tribe is owned by Grace and Skip Llewelllyn. Grace is the author of *The Teenage Liberation Handbook* (new edition coming in 1998).

Hewitt Homeschooling Resources
P.O. Box 9
Washougal, WA 98671
Phone: 1-800-348-1750 (information)
        (360) 835-8708 (orders)
Fax: (360) 835-8697
E-mail: hewitths@aol.com

Distribution area   National

Religious affiliation   Nondenominational

Age levels served   Preschool–18 (PreS–grade 12)

Materials provided   Parent support; curriculum materials; educational enrichment materials; homeschooling information/publications

Subject specialty   Special needs and high school for home school

Holt Associates/John Holt's Book and Music Store
2269 Massachusetts Avenue
Cambridge, MA 02140-1226
Phone: (617) 864-3100 (information and orders)
Fax: (617) 864-9235
E-mail: HoltGWS@aol.com
Web site: http://www.holtGWS.com

Distribution area   National

Religious affiliation   None

Age levels served   Preschool–18 (PreS–grade 12)

Materials provided   Parent support; educational enrichment materials (games, software, flashcards, etc.); homeschooling information/publications; magazine: *Growing without Schooling* (6 issues/year); legislation information; consultations; seminars

Subject specialty   Homeschooling without fixed curriculum

Home Education Magazine's Homeschooling Information & Resource Guide
P.O. Box 1083
Tonasket, WA 98855
Phone: (509) 586-1351
E-mail: HomeEdMag@aol.com

Distribution area   National

Religious affiliation   None

Materials provided   Parent support; homeschooling information/publications; educational enrichment materials (including software); magazine (see *Home Education Magazine* listing); lists of support groups and organizations

Subject specialty   Homeschooling

Statement   This is a free, 24-page publication that can be used to inform others about homeschooling. In addition to information about resources (books, magazines, software, correspondence programs), this guide includes articles on homeschooling and Q's and A's on homeschooling issues.

Homeschool Support Network
P.O. Box 708
Gray, ME 04039
Phone: (207) 657-2800
Fax: (207) 657-2404
E-mail: HSN@outrig.com
Web site: www.outrig.com/familytimes

Distribution area   National (Additional offices in Michigan and Colorado)

Religious affiliation   Christian-based; open to all homeschoolers

Age levels served   Preschool–18 (PreS–grade 12)

Materials provided   Parent support; curriculum materials; educational enrichment materials; homeschooling information; magazine: *Home Educator's Family Times* (5 issues/year); consultation; referrals; conferences

Subject specialty   Offers information, advice, referrals, help finding support groups, resources, and more

Latter-Day Family Resources
140 N. Main Street
Spanish Fork, UT 84660
Phone: (801) 798-2106 (Monday–Saturday, 9:30–5:30 MST)
        1-800-290-2283 (24-hour toll free; orders only)
Fax: (801) 798-2067
E-mail (orders only): orders@ldfr.com
        (questions): questions@ldfr.com
Web site: http://www.ldfr.com

Distribution area   National

Religious affiliation   Latter-Day Saints

Materials provided   Curriculum materials; educational enrichment materials; newsletter: *Latter-Day Family* (6 issues/year)

Subject specialty   "Unique products not found elsewhere. Run by a homeschooling family."

Laurelwood Publications
Rt. 1, Box 878
Bluemont, VA 20135
Phone: (540) 554-2500
Fax: (540) 554-2938
E-mail: Laurelwood@juno.com
Contact person: Mary Ellen

Distribution area   National

Religious affiliation   None

Age levels served   Preschool–18 (PreS–grade 12)

Materials provided   Curriculum; curriculum resources; homeschooling information; catalog available

Subject specialty   Used curriculum, but also many new products

The Learning Parent
Rt. 3, Box 543
Rustburg, VA 24588
Phone: (804) 845-8345
Fax: (804) 845-8345
Contact person: Rick or Marilyn Boyer

Distribution area   National

Religious affiliation   Christian

Age levels served   Preschool–18 (PreS–grade 12)

Materials provided   Parent support and materials (including cassette tape series); curriculum (including *Proverbs Character Curriculum*);

homeschooling information; seminars; speakers for home education conventions

Subject specialty Homeschooling information—encouragement, teaching and child-rearing information for parents who are home educating their children. The Boyers are authors of six books on home education, and they offer a nine-hour seminar for homeschooling conferences.

Learning Resources Distributing Centre
12360 142 Street, N.W.
Edmonton, Alberta T5L 4X9 Canada
Phone: (403) 427-2767 (information)
        (403) 427-5775 (orders)
Fax: (403) 422-9750
E-mail: sjones@lrdc.edc.gov.ab.ca
Web site: http://ednet.edc.gov.ab.ca/lrdc
Contact person: Sharee Jones, Customer Service and Marketing Manager

Distribution area Alberta Province

Religious affiliation None

Age levels served 5–18 (K–grade 12)

Materials provided Complete curriculum; textbooks; curriculum enrichment materials; parent support; testing; Buyers Guide available in print format or on LRDC's Web site.

Subject specialty Alberta Education authorized, approved, and/or developed learning resources that are used to meet Alberta Education's learning objectives as outlined in Alberta's Curriculum. The LRDC also sells general learning resources that are in high demand by teachers, such as maps, atlases, globes, dictionaries, manuals, and classroom reference materials.

The Moore Foundation
Box 1
Camas, WA 98607
Phone: (360) 835-5500 (information)
        (360) 835-2736 (orders)
Fax: (360) 835-5392

E-mail: moorefnd@pacifier.com
Web site: http://www.caslink.com/moorefoundation

Distribution area   National

Religious affiliation   Independent (Moores are Seventh-day Adventists)

Age levels served   Preschool–18 (PreS–grade 12)

Materials provided   Parent support; curriculum materials; educational enrichment materials; homeschooling information/publications; newsletter: *Moore Report International* (6 issues/year); legislation information; special needs; research; booklist available

Subject specialty   Materials written and chosen by Ray and Dorothy Moore. The Moores are well known for their belief in a well-rounded education, which includes service to the community, for their inspiring books on home education, and for their research on homeschooling issues.

Sycamore Tree Catalog
2179 Meyer Place
Costa Mesa, CA 92627
Phone: (714) 650-4466 (information)
          1-800-779-6750 (orders)
Fax: (714) 642-6750
E-mail: 75767.1417@compuserve.com
Web site: http://www.sycamoretree.com

Distribution area   National

Religious affiliation   Nonsectarian Christian

Age levels served   Preschool–18 (PreS–grade 12)

Materials provided   Complete curriculum; specialized curriculum; textbooks; curriculum enrichment materials (games, art/craft supplies, dollhouse supplies; science materials and equipment, etc.); Bible-based material; parent support; homeschooling information/publications; newsletter (10 issues/year); free catalog available

Subject specialty   Curriculum and curriculum enrichment materials

Timberdoodle Company
E. 1510 Spencer Lake Road
Shelton, WA 98584
Phone: (360) 426-0672 (information and orders)
Fax: (360) 427-5625
E-mail: mailbag@timberdoodle.com
Web site: http://www.timberdoodle.com

Distribution area   National

Religious affiliation   Christian

Age levels served   Preschool–18 (PreS–grade 12)

Materials provided   Parent support; educational enrichment materials

Homeschooling
Periodicals

The Adventist Home Educator
P.O. Box 836
Camino, CA 95709
Phone: (916) 647-2110
Editor: Judy Shewmake

Distribution area: National

Religious affiliation: Seventh-day Adventist

Type of publication: Newsletter

Issues/year: 12

Subscription price: $10.00/year; $.50/single copy

Content   Letters from readers; editorials; pen pals; learning projects; curriculum and book reviews; Q's & A's; swap-n-shop; teen talk; kids corner; family experiences re homeschooling

Purpose of publication   Information and support for Seventh-day Adventist parents who are educating their children at home

Aero-Gramme
417 Roslyn Road
Roslyn Heights, NY 11577
Phone: (516) 621-2195

Fax: (516) 625-3257
E-mail: jmintz@igc.apc.org
Editor: Jerry Mintz

Distribution area: National
Religious affiliation: None
Type of publication: Newsletter
Subscription price: $15.00/year

Purpose of publication   The newsletter of the Alternative Education Resource Organization of the School of Living (AERO), Jerry Mintz, Director, *Aero-Gramme* is a newsletter about alternative education.

The AHA Online Newsletter
E-mail: AHAonline@aol.com
Web site: http://www.home-ed-press.com/AHA_inf.html

Distribution area: National
Religious affiliation: None
Type of publication: Online newsletter
Issues/year: 12
Subscription price: Free upon request; to subscribe, send E-mail
                message with your E-mail address to:
                AHAonline@aol.com
                Back issues can be downloaded from the AHA
                Web site (listed above).

Content   News, articles, press releases, reviews, access to over 100 files maintained by the American Homeschool Association, including laws and information files for all fifty states

Purpose of publication   "To inform, support, and educate parents and anyone interested in homeschooling"

A Call to Closeness
Latter-Day Saints Home Educators' Association
2770 South 1000 West
Perry, UT 84302
Phone: (801) 723-5355

Distribution area: National

Religious affiliation: Latter-Day Saint

Type of publication: Newsletter

Issues/year: 4

Subscription price: $8.00/year

Content   Contact with other homeschooling parents, resources, parenting information, relating the gospel to homeschooling, product coupons

Purpose of publication   "The LDS–HEA provides support and information to parents, particularly those outside of Utah, who wish to take full responsibility for the education of their children." The newsletter helps to bring the worldwide group of LDS homeschoolers together.

Family Explorer
6874 East Harvard Avenue
Denver, CO 80224-2505
Phone: (303) 691-2172 (information and orders)
E-mail: starman@usa.net
Web site: http://members.aol.com/fenews/index.htm
Editor: Larry Sessions

Distribution area: National

Religious affiliation: None

Age level: 6–12 years

Type of publication: Newsletter (Subtitle: *Parents and Kids Exploring Nature Together*)

Issues/year: 12

Subscription price: $16.95/year; publication is available in print and online

Content   "The emphasis is on seasonal activities and projects parents can use to introduce their kids to a variety of science and nature topics. No special equipment is needed, and activities can be adapted to a range of ages." Four to eight activities are provided each month, along with a star chart and word puzzle.

Purpose of publication   Activities and/or articles included are intended specifically for adults who have little or no background in science. Larry Sessions worked with the Denver Museum of Natural History for twelve years before leaving to begin this newsletter.

FLExOnline
Family Learning Exchange
E-mail: FmlyLrngEx@aol.com
Web site: http://www.olywa.net/flex
Editor: Janie Levine Hellyer

Distribution area: National

Religious affiliation: None

Type of publication: Online newsletter

Issues/year: 21 (2/month during the school year; 1/month in summer)

Subscription price: Free; to subscribe, send an E-mail message to
FmlyLrngEx@aol.com with "Subscribe
FLExOnline" in the subject line.
Back issues can be found at the FLExOnline Web
site.

Content News items pertinent to homeschoolers; feature stories; information about upcoming conferences and other events for home-schoolers around the country; letters and responses from homeschool-ing parents on various topics of concern; short reviews of computer software and Internet sites

Purpose of the publication "Written and edited by parents and others interested in natural learning and homeschooling, FLExOnline pro-vides networking, support, information, and news to the homeschool community."

F.U.N. News (Family Unschoolers Network)
1688 Belhaven Woods Court
Pasadena, MD 21122-3727
Phone: (410) 360-7330 (information and orders)
Fax: (410) 360-7330
E-mail: FUNNews @MCImail.com
Web site: http://members.aol.com/FUNNews
Editors: Nancy and Billy Greer

Distribution area: International

Religious affiliation: None

Type of publication: Newsletter

Issues/year: 4

Subscription price: $8.00/year; $2.50/single copy
Free sample upon request, also available on Web site.

Content Articles on homeschooling issues; reviews of books, software, and other materials; information about homeschooling organizations; information about new educational opportunities/resources, such as spelling bees, art materials, publications, and lists of suppliers; information about upcoming conferences around the country; letters from readers, columns, artwork, ads. Each issue has a theme focus (e.g., socialization, math, thrift, genealogy).

Purpose of publication "To provide families with ideas on how learning can be fun, and to promote the belief that learning is a lifelong process."

Growing Without Schooling
Holt Associates
2269 Massachusetts Avenue
Cambridge, MA 02140-1226
Phone: (617) 864-3100 (information and orders)
Fax: (617) 864-9235
E-mail: HoltGWS@aol.com
Web site: http://www.holtGWS.com
Editor: Susannah Sheffer

Distribution area: International

Religious affiliation: None

Type of publication: Magazine

Issues/year: 6

Subscription price: $25.00/year; $6.00/single copy
$29.00/year Canada
$40.00/year airmail outside of North America;
$29.00 surface mail (allow 2–3 months)

Content "Primarily letters between parents and children engaged in homeschooling; interviews with educators and authors; reviews and resource listings."

Purpose of publication "To promote homeschooling, in general and to the public, and the ideas of John Holt in particular."

Home Education Magazine
P.O. Box 1587
Palmer, AK 99645
Phone: (907) 746-1334 (information)
      1-800-236-3278 (orders)
Fax: (907) 746-1335
E-mail: HomeEdmag@aol.com
Web site: http://www.home-ed-press.com
Editors: Mark and Helen Hegener

Distribution area: International

Religious affiliation: None

Type of publicaton: Magazine; also, the HEM Online Newsletter is available free to anyone with an E-mail account. Contact HEMnewsltr@aol.com for details or visit the HEM Web site (listed above).

Issues/year: 6

Subscription price: $24.00/year; $4.50/single copy
      $39.00/year (U.S. funds) Canada

Content Articles, columns, news, reviews, interviews with homeschooling personalities; information about organizations and companies offering products and services for homeschoolers; letters from readers; information about Web sites of various homeschooling organizations; movie reviews; a networking section, which includes pen pals, homeschooling parents, conference information, information on international, national, state, and local homeschooling organizations, and ads

Purpose of publication Homeschooling information, articles, and support

Home Educator's *Family Times*
Homeschool Support Network
P.O. Box 708
Gray, ME 04039
Phone: (207) 657-2800
Fax: (207) 657-2404
E-mail: familytimes@outrig.com
Web site: http://www.outrig.com/familytimes
Editor: Jane R. Boswell

Distribution area: National

Religious affiliation: Christian-based; open to all homeschoolers

Type of publication: Magazine

Issues/year: 5

Subscription price: $15.00/year

Content Educational articles; informational research-based articles of interest to parents and home educators, ads

Purpose of publication "To support, inform, educate and encourage families seeking to educate their own children."

Homefires: The Journal of Homeschooling
180 El Camino Real, Suite #10
Millbrae, CA 94030
Phone: 1-888-4-HOME-ED (1-888-446-6663) toll free (information
    and orders)
E-mail: Editor@Homefires.com
Web site: http://www.Homefires.com
Editor: Diane Flynn Keith

Distribution area: Statewide

Religious affiliation: None

Type of publication: Magazine

Issues/year: 6

Subscription price: $27.95/year; $5.00/single copy

Content Articles on various aspects of homeschooling (and regarding various ages of children) by well-known voices in the home school education community; open-ended curriculum enhancement, with activities in each branch of study (history, science, math, reading, etc.); educational resource reviews; online and educational software reviews; information on upcoming events, field trips, classes, and support groups throughout California and beyond

Purpose of publication "To provide support and networking, information, and resources for families who choose to educate children at home."

Home School Court Report
Home School Legal Defense Association
P.O. Box 3000
Purcellville, VA 20132
Phone: (540) 338-5600
E-mail: mailroom@hslda.org
Web site: http://www.hslda.org

Distribution area: National

Religious affiliation: Christian background, but serves everyone

Type of publication: Newsletter

Issues/year: 6

Subscription price: $15.00/year

Content Legal information and news of interest to homeschoolers

Home School Digest
Wisdom's Gate/Home School Digest
P.O. Box 3746
Covert, MI 49043
Phone: 1-800-343-1943 (orders)
Fax: (616) 764-1710

Distribution area: National

Religious affiliation: Christian

Type of publication: Journal (Subtitle: *The Quarterly Journal for Serious Home-schoolers*)

Issues/year: 4

Subscription price: $18.00/year; $5.00/single copy

Content Covers numerous subjects related to the homeschooling lifestyle in in-depth articles. (The journal is nearly 100 pages per issue.) Also includes product reviews, resource directory, and ads.

Purpose of publication "We appeal especially to serious scholarly parents. The publication is designed to encourage and equip parents. Emphasis on developing a Biblical worldview, family discipleship, character building."

Home School Helper
Bob Jones University Press
Greenville, SC 29614-0060
Phone: (864) 242-5100 (information)
         1-800-845-5731 (orders)
Fax: (864) 298-0268
E-mail: bjup@bju.edu
Web site: http://www.bju.edu/press
Editor: Mark Sidwell

Distribution area: National

Religious affiliation: Nondenominational Protestant

Type of Publication: Newsletter

Issues/year: 4

Subscription price: Free—available in print and online

Content   Informational articles; updates on materials; publications, services, conferences sponsored by Bob Jones University; ads

Purpose of publication   "To provide informational articles on home school issues, teacher helps, and educational hints to help parents give their children the best education possible."

Home School Researcher
National Home Education Research Institute
P.O. Box 13939
Salem, OR 97309
Phone: (503) 364-1490
Fax: (503) 364-2827
E-mail: mail@nheri.org
Web site: http://www.nheri.org
Editor: Brian D. Ray

Distribution area: National

Religious affiliation: None

Type of publication: Journal (refereed)

Issues/year: 4

Subscription price: $25.00/year individual; $40.00/year library or
              organization

Content Publishes research related to home education; articles on demographics of homeschoolers, homeschooling issues, achievements, etc.

Purpose of publication Helps to fulfill the mission of the National Home Education Research Institute by "educating the public concerning the findings of all research on home education"

Homeschooling Today
P.O. Box 1608
Fort Collins, CO 80522-1608
Phone: (954) 962-1930 (information and orders)
Fax: (954) 964-7466
Editors: Debbie and Greg Strayer

Distribution area: International

Religious affiliation: Christian

Type of publication: Magazine (Subtitle: *Practical Help for Christian Families*)

Issues/year: 6

Subscription price: $19.99/year; $5.95/single copy

Content Feature articles; information on resources; columns; book reviews; unit study; curriculum; homeschooling problems and advice; product reviews; religious articles; ads

Purpose of publication "Encouragement and curriculum ideas for homeschooling."

Latter-Day Family
140 North Main
Spanish Fork, UT 84660
Phone: (801) 798-2106 (information and orders)
        1-800-290-2283 (orders only)
Fax: (801) 798-2067
E-mail: orders@ldfr.com
Web site: http://www.ldfr.com/newslt.html

Distribution area: National

Religious affiliation: Latter-Day Saint

Type of publication: Newsletter

Issues/year: 6

Subscription price: $12.00/year

Content   Feature articles on homeschooling, gardening, herbal medicine; recipes for nutritious meals; daily gospel living, child raising, etc.

The Learning Edge
Clonlara School
1289 Jewett
Ann Arbor, MI 48104

Distribution area: National

Religious affiliation: None

Type of publication: Newsletter

Issues/year: 5

Subscription price: $15.00/year

Content   Resources; announcements; feature articles from the director; learning tips; regional news; Support Corner; student writings

Purpose of publication   "To educate and update our homeschooling families with newsworthy information."

The Link: A Homeschool Newspaper
587 N. Ventu Park Road
Newbury Park, CA 91320
Phone: (805) 492-1373
Fax: (805) 493-9216
E-mail: hompaper@gte.net
Web site: http://www.conejovalley.com/thelink
Editor/Publisher: Mary Leppert

Religious affiliation: None

Issued: Bimonthly (since 1995)

Subscription price: Free

Purpose   "To provide information and resources free to those homeschooling and/or interested in homeschooling, and to do so without promoting an agenda relative to religion, spiritual belief/non-belief or homeschooling style."

Statement *The Link* "provides a broad variety of services, resources and information to all homeschoolers." Articles relate to various aspects of homeschooling and education. Many ads are included. This newspaper accepts submissions of all kinds relating to homeschooling from parents and children, including those on a list of topics suggested in the newspaper's "Writer's Guidelines." The Web site includes articles from back issues of the publication, as well as links to other homeschooling resources and information regarding *The Link's* annual homeschool conference.

Living Education
Oak Meadow School
P.O. Box 1712
Blacksburg, VA 24063
Phone: (540) 552-3263

Distribution area: National
Religious affiliation: None
Type of publication: Newsletter
Issues/year: 6
Subscription price: $18.00/year

Content Articles on children, parenting, learning, alternative healing and natural living, and on homeschooling; poems and stories by children; variety of authors; book reviews; resources

Moore Report International
The Moore Foundation
Box 1
Camas, WA 98607
Phone: (360) 835-5500 (information)
       (360) 835-2736 (orders)
Fax: (360) 835-5392
E-mail: moorefnd@pacifier.com
Web site: http://www.caslink.com/moorefoundation
Editors: Dr. Raymond and Dorothy Moore

Distribution area: International

Religious affiliation: Independent (Moores are Seventh-day Adventists)

Type of publication: Newsletter

Issues/year: 6

Subscription price: $12.00/year

Content   Articles about homeschooling families and accomplishments of home schooled children of various ages; feature article by Raymond Moore; editorial by Dorothy Moore; articles on educational issues; "Health Nuggets"; information on upcoming seminars; letters to the editor, and more.

Purpose of publication   To continue and professionalize high quality, all-around education as emphasized by the Moores.

NATHHAN News
National Challenged Homeschoolers
5383 Alpine Road, S. E.
Olalla, WA 98359
Phone: (253) 857-4257
Fax: (253) 857-7764
E-mail: NATHANEWS@aol.com
Editor: Tom Bushnell

Distribution area: National

Religious affiliation: Christian

Type of publication: Newsletter

Issues/year: 4

Subscription price: Included with membership in NATHHAN:
$25.00/year; $35.00/year Canada or overseas
Back issues available for $3.75 each

Content   Letters and articles from families homeschooling special needs children; tips from professionals; information on new teaching methods, products and organizations; inspiring stories; encouragement and help

Purpose of publication   "A Christ centered magazine for families teaching special needs children at home"

Options in Learning
Alliance for Parental Involvement in Education (ALLPIE)
P.O. Box 59
East Chatham, NY 12060-0059
Phone: (518) 392-6900
E-mail: allpie@taconic.net

Distribution area: National

Religious affiliation: None

Type of publication: Newsletter

Issues/year: 4

Subscription price: $20.00/year

Content   Letters from homeschooling families; calendar of upcoming events/conferences of alternative education organizations; book reviews of books on educational issues; parenting topics; a feature article

Pennsylvania Homeschoolers Newsletter
R.R. 2, Box 117
Kittanning, PA 16201-9311
Phone: (412) 783-6512
Fax: (412) 783-6852
Editors: Howard and Susan Richman

Distribution area: National

Religious affiliation: None

Type of publication: Newsletter

Issues/year: 4

Subscription price: $12.00/year

Content   Personal stories by homeschooling parents and children; reviews of homeschooling resources; updates on legal issues regarding homeschooling in Pennsylvania; support group listings; phone directory; calendar of major events; children's writings

Practical Homeschooling
Home Life
P.O. Box 1250
Fenton, MO 63026-1850

Phone: 1-800-346-6322 (orders)
Fax: (314) 225-0743
E-mail: 73014.644@compuserve.com
        practic@aol.com (for letters & articles)
Editor: Mary Pride

Distribution area: National
Religious affiliation: Christian
Type of publication: Newsletter
Issues/year: 4
Subscription price: $15.00/year; $25.00/year Canada

Content   Articles on various subjects; product reviews, teaching methods; detailed information about using computers in homeschooling; college information; many ads

Purpose of publication   Emphasis on learning materials

The Teaching Home
Box 20219
Portland, OR 97294-0219
Phone: (503) 253-9633
        1-800-395-7760
Editors: Pat and Sue Welch

Distribution area: National
Religious affiliation: Christian
Type of publication: Magazine
Issues/year: 6
Subscription price: $15.00/year

Content   Home education news; articles; letters from readers; calendars of state and national events; newsletter inserts from a home education organization in your state and a neighboring state; practical teaching tips; in-depth articles on a specific subject in each issue

Purpose of publication   "To provide information, inspiration, and support to Christian home-school families and Christian homeschool state and national organizations."

Bibliography

The following bibliography, while not intended to be an exhaustive list, does include a large number of important books and articles about the homeschooling movement and the home education of children. Also included is a selection of titles, arranged by subject, that illustrates the type of material that is frequently requested by homeschooling parents and their children. It is a basic collection of books, many of them generally available in public library collections, that can be used as a foundation for service to the homeschooling community.

Articles on Homeschooling

Avner, Jane A. "Home Schoolers: A Forgotten Clientele?" *School Library Journal* (July 1989): 29.

Churbuck, David C. "The Ultimate School Choice: No School at All." *Forbes,* October 11, 1993, 145–50.

Cook, Anthony. "When Your Home Is the Classroom." *Money,* September 1991, 105.

Dunleavy, M. P. "Staying Close to Home." *Publishers Weekly* 242, no. 29 (July 17, 1993): 142–44.

Farenga, Patrick. "Homeschooling in the 90's." *Mothering,* Fall 1996, 56–63.

Gibbs, Nancy. "Home Sweet School." *Time,* October 31, 1994, 62–63.

Kennedy, John W. "Home Schooling Grows Up." *Christianity Today,* July 1, 1995, 50–52.

Klipsch, Pamela R. "An Educated Collection for Homeschoolers." *Library Journal* 120, no. 2 (February 1, 1995): 47.

LaRue, James and Suzanne LaRue. "Is Anybody Home? Home Schooling and the Library." *Wilson Library Bulletin,* September 1991, 23.

Lines, Patricia M. "Home Schooling." *ERIC Digest,* no. 95 (EDO–EA–95–3) April 1995.

Lines, Patricia M. "An Overview of Home Instruction." *Phi Delta Kappan* 68 (1987): 510–17.

Lockwood, Annette. "Bookmobile Provides Homeschoolers with Regular Library Period." *American Libraries* 27, no. 10 (November 1996) 32–33.

Madden, Susan B. "Learning at Home: Public Library Service to Home Schoolers." *School Library Journal* 37, no. 7 (July 1991): 23–25.

Roorbach, Bill. "Mommy, What's a Classroom?" *The New York Times Magazine,* February 2, 1997, 30–37.

Rupp, Becky. "Home Schooling." *Country Journal,* December 1986, 67.

Sager, Don, et al. "Public Library Service to Homeschoolers." *Public Libraries* 34, no. 4 (July/August 1995): 201–5.

Schnaiberg, Lynn. "Staying Home from School." *Education Week* 15, no. 38 (June 12, 1996): 24–33.

Stecklow, Steve. "Fed Up with Schools, More Parents Turn to Teaching at Home." *Wall Street Journal,* May 10, 1994, sec. A1, 2.

Viadero, Debra. "Home-Schooled Pupils Outscore Counterparts." *Education Week on the Web,* March 19, 1997.

Books

Homeschooling: Introduction, History, and Fundamentals

Colfax, David, and Micki Colfax. *Homeschooling for Excellence.* New York: Warner Books, 1988.

> The Colfaxes have written of their experiences homeschooling their four sons, including the methods and materials they used.

Crow, Alexis. *Home Education: Rights and Reasons.* Wheaton, Ill.: Crossway Books, 1993.

> Crow is legal coordinator for the Rutherford Institute.

Gorder, Cheryl. *Home Schools: An Alternative,* 4th ed. Mesa, Ariz.: Blue Bird Publishing, 1996.

Why parents should or should not choose to home educate their children: legal, religious, social, educational, and psychological aspects. Includes lists of resources.

Guterson, David. *Family Matters: Why Homeschooling Makes Sense.* San Diego: Harcourt Brace, 1993.

A high school English teacher who home schools his own children, the author looks at both worlds, giving strong, realistic justifications for homeschooling and ideas for cooperation between families and schools.

Hegener, Mark, and Helen Hegener. *The Home School Reader,* 2nd rev. ed. Tonasket, Wash.: Home Education Press, 1995.

A collection of articles by many authors from *Home Education Magazine,* 1984–1994, on topics such as socialization, homeschooling laws, and choosing curriculum.

Holt, John. *Learning All the Time.* New York: Addison-Wesley, 1989.

"How small children begin to read, write, count, and investigate the world without being taught." Holt discusses how children learn, from everyday activities, to make more sense of the world around them and indicates through discussion and personal anecdotes how adults can help, rather than hinder, this process.

Klicka, Christopher. *The Right Choice: Home Schooling.* Gresham, Ore.: Noble Publishing, 1995.

Practical reasons and legal justifications for schooling your children at home produced by Christian Life Workshops. Klicka is Senior Counsel of the Home School Legal Defense Association.

Lurie, Jon. *Allison's Story: A Book about Homeschooling.* Minneapolis: Lerner Publications, 1996.

A brief photo essay describing the homeschooling experiences of an eight-year-old girl and her family.

Moore, Raymond. *School Can Wait.* Provo, Utah: Brigham Young University Press, 1979.

A defense of delayed formal education based on ten years of research studies.

Schooling at Home: Parents, Kids and Learning, ed. by Anne Pedersen and Peggy O'Mara. Santa Fe, N.M.: John Muir Publications, 1990.

> Excerpts from *Mothering Magazine* regarding learning, legal issues, and home education—some articles by recognized leaders in homeschool education.

Shackelford, Luanne, and Susan White. *A Survivor's Guide to Home Schooling.* Westchester, Ill.: Crossway Books, 1988.

> Time constraints, respectability of home education, teaching, and testing are discussed from the Christian point of view for prospective homeschoolers.

Voetberg, Julie. *I Am a Home Schooler.* Morton Grove, Ill.: Albert Whitman, 1995.

> A short, first-person account of a home-schooled nine-year-old girl's education and family life.

Wade, Theodore, E. Jr. *School at Home: How Parents Can Teach Their Own Children.* Colfax, Calif.: Gazelle Publications, 1980.

> A thorough and honest study of the dangers and strengths of teaching children at home.

Whitehead, John W., and Alexis Crow. *Home Education: Rights and Reasons.* Wheaton, Ill.: Crossway Books, 1993.

> Historical, legal, and educational perspectives on homeschooling.

Homeschooling: How-to

Farenga, Patrick. *The Beginner's Guide to Homeschooling,* rev. ed. Cambridge, Mass.: Holt Associates, 1997.

> Offers questions and thorough answers about homeschooling, choosing a curriculum, evaluating achievement, keeping records. Includes lists of state support groups, correspondence schools, materials, and more.

Hegener, Mark, and Helen Hegener. *Alternatives in Education: Family Choices in Learning.* Tonasket, Wash.: Home Education Press, 1987.

> Concrete suggestions for getting started in homeschooling.

Hegener, Mark, and Helen Hegener. *Homeschool Handbook.* Tonasket, Wash.: Home Education Press, 1994.

Hendrickson, Borg. *Home School: Taking the First Step*. Sitka, Alaska: Mountain Meadow Press, 1994.

Fundamental questions about homeschooling are answered in this practical, up-to-date guide.

Hendrickson, Borg. *How to Write a Low-Cost/No-Cost Curriculum for Your Home-School Child,* rev. ed. Sitka, Alaska: Mountain Meadow Press, 1995.

Hensley, Sharon C. *Home Schooling Children with Special Needs.* Gresham, Ore.: Noble Publishing Associates, 1995.

Based on her own knowledge and experience, Hensley defines the various types of learning disabilities, discusses various stumbling blocks faced by prospective homeschoolers, and offers advice on planning a program for your child.

Hirsch, E. D. Jr., Editor-in-Chief. The Core Knowledge Series. New York: Bantam Doubleday Dell 1992–1997.

The Core Knowledge Series offers an exciting approach to learning the fundamentals of the major academic subjects, which are arranged in a way that encourages parent or teacher and child to make connections between the disciplines, providing "the foundation for further learning." Individual titles are:

Books to Build On: A Grade-by-Grade Resource Guide for Parents and Teachers, ed. E. D. Hirsch Jr., Core Knowledge Foundation, and John Holdren. New York: Delta, 1996.

What Your Fifth Grader Needs to Know: Fundamentals of a Good Fifth-grade Education, ed. E. D. Hirsch Jr., New York: Doubleday, 1993.

What Your First Grader Needs to Know: Fundamentals of a Good First-grade Education, ed. E. D. Hirsch Jr., New York: Doubleday, 1997.

What Your Fourth Grader Needs to Know: Fundamentals of a Good Fourth-grade Education, ed. E. D. Hirsch Jr. New York: Doubleday, 1992.

What Your Kindergartner Needs to Know: Preparing Your Child for a Lifetime of Learning, ed. E. D. Hirsch Jr. and John Holdren. New York: Doubleday, 1996.

What Your Second Grader Needs to Know: Fundamentals of a Good Second-grade Education, ed. E. D. Hirsch Jr. New York: Doubleday, 1991.

What Your Sixth Grader Needs to Know: Fundamentals of a Good Sixth-grade Education, ed. E. D. Hirsch Jr. New York: Doubleday, 1993.

What Your Third Grader Needs to Know: Fundamentals of a Good Third-grade Education, ed. E. D. Hirsch Jr. New York: Doubleday, 1992.

Holt, John. *Teach Your Own: A Hopeful Path for Education.* New York: Delacorte, 1981.

> Holt emphasizes involving children in their own learning process.

Hood, Mary. *The Relaxed Home School: A Family Production.* Tempe, Ariz.: Ambleside Educational Press, 1994.

> A beginner's guide to creating your own less-structured curriculum by a homeschooling mom and teacher, from a Christian perspective.

Hubbs, Don. *Home Education Resource Guide,* 4th ed. Mesa, Ariz.: Blue Bird Publishing, 1996.

> This beginner's guide to curriculum resources, updated on a regular basis, includes conservative Christian, alternative, holistic, and libertarian perspectives on homeschooling.

Kaseman, M. Larry, and Susan D. Kaseman. *Taking Charge Through Homeschooling.* Stoughton, Wis.: Koshkenong Press, 1990.

> This basic primer on homeschooling offers information and advice on topics such as alternative approaches to learning; record-keeping; forming/joining support groups; legal and other challenges facing homeschoolers.

McIntire, Deborah, and Robert Windham. *Home Schooling: Answers to Questions Parents Most Often Ask.* Cypress, Calif.: Creative Teaching Press, 1995.

> Two educators who are currently home education consultants offer a short, encouraging, practical introduction to the how and why of homeschooling. Includes good coverage of Canadian resources.

Moore, Dorothy, and Raymond Moore. *The Successful Homeschool Family Handbook: A Creative and Stressfree Approach to Homeschooling.* Nashville, Tenn.: Thomas Nelson, 1994.

> The Moores offer guidelines for putting together a homeschool curriculum that avoids parent and student burnout. Their Moore Formula emphasizes the child's needs and interests, creativity, community/family service, high achievement, sociability, and low cost. Includes advice and success stories from effective homeschoolers.

Pride, Mary. *Big Book of Home Learning,* 4 vols. Wheaton, Ill.: Crossway Books, 1990–91.

> A guide to educational materials and resources of all types and homeschooling basics for every age, from preschool through adult. Includes many Christian educational supplies.

Rupp, Rebecca. *Good Stuff: Learning Tools for All Ages,* rev. ed. Tonasket, Wash.: Home Education Press, 1997.

> A comprehensive collection of learning resources, organized by subject.

Wade, Theodore, et al. *The Home School Manual: Plans, Pointers, Reasons and Resources for Parents Who Teach Their Own Children,* 6th ed. Bridgman, Mich.: Gazelle Publications, 1996.

> This regularly updated sourcebook offers general guidelines for Christian homeschoolers as well as suggestions on how to teach various subjects.

Teaching Techniques

Amerikaner, Susan. *101 Things to Do to Develop Your Child's Gifts and Talents.* New York: Tom Doherty Associates, 1989.

> Emphasizing critical and creative thinking skills, the author suggests activities for children aged six through nine that will help to cultivate their natural abilities.

Armstrong, Thomas. *Awakening Your Child's Natural Genius: Enhancing Curiosity, Creativity, and Learning Ability.* Los Angeles: Jeremy P. Tarcher, 1991.

> This book is filled with resources and practical suggestions to enable parents of children aged three to twelve to recognize their own gifts and talents.

Caney, Steven. *Steven Caney's Play Book.* New York: Workman Publishing, 1975.

Projects, constructions, games, puzzles, and other activities for children organized according to the spaces where they play; inexpensive household materials are used creatively to stimulate the child's imagination.

Gordon, Thomas. *Teaching Children Through Self-discipline at Home and at School: New ways for parents and teachers to build self-confidence, self-esteem, and self-reliance.* New York: Times Books, 1989.

The author of *Parent Effectiveness Training* offers a nontraditional method for changing children's behavior through cooperation.

Hendricks, Gay, and Thomas B. Roberts. *The Second Centering Book.* Englewood Cliffs, N.J.: Prentice-Hall, 1987.

Provides awareness activities for children and parents for relaxing the body and mind.

Jones, Claudia. *Parents Are Teachers, Too: Enriching Your Child's First Six Years.* Charlotte, Vt.: Williamson Publishing, 1988.

Activities, problem-solving techniques, basic learning skills that parents can provide to help their young children on the road to creative thinking.

Jones, Claudia. *More Parents Are Teachers, Too: Encouraging Your Six-to Twelve-Year-Old.* Charlotte, Vt.: Williamson Publishing, 1990.

Includes practical exercises and activities in math and writing skills, perceptive observation, computers, and researching ideas that encourage a love of learning.

Kealoha, Anna. *Trust the Children: A Manual and Activity Guide for Homeschooling and Alternative Learning.* Berkeley, Calif.: Celestial Arts, 1995.

A compendium of activities and games, covering a wide variety of subjects (the usual, plus many others, such as meditation, friendship, libraries, public speaking) that parents can use to make learning exciting for their children.

Singer, Dorothy G. *The Parent's Guide: Use TV to Your Child's Advantage.* Reston, Va.: Acropolis, 1990.

Suggestions for using television in the home to help children develop critical thinking skills.

Speitz, Heide Anne. *Modern Montessori at Home: A Creative Teaching Guide for Parents of Children Six through Nine Years of Age.* Rossmoor, Calif.: American Montessori Consulting, 1989.

Techniques for making reading and writing, spelling, science, and geography fun for your child.

———. *Modern Montessori at Home II: A Creative Teaching Guide for Parents of Children Ten through Twelve Years of Age.* Rossmoor, Calif.: American Montessori Consulting, 1990.

———. *Montessori at Home: A Complete Guide to Teaching Your Preschooler at Home Using the Montessori Method.* Rossmoor, Calif.: American Montessori Consulting, 1991.

Using Literature in the Home Classroom

Barstow, Barbara, and Judy Riggle. *Beyond Picture Books: A Guide to First Readers,* 2nd ed. Providence, N.J.: Bowker, 1995.

The finest easy readers available are annotated in this select bibliography.

Carroll, Frances Laverne, and Mary Meacham. *Exciting, Funny, Scary, Short, Different, and Sad Books Kids Like About Animals, Science, Sports, Families, Songs, and Other Things.* Chicago: American Library Association, 1984.

———. *More Exciting, Funny, Scary, Short, Different, and Sad Books Kids Like About Animals, Science, Sports, Families, Songs, and Other Things.* Chicago: American Library Association, 1992.

Both volumes include annotated lists of children's books on topics kids request, both fiction and nonfiction.

Freeman, Judy. *Books Kids Will Sit Still For: The Complete Read-aloud Guide,* 2nd ed. New York: Bowker, 1992.

———. *More Books Kids Will Sit Still For: A Read-aloud Guide.* New Providence, N.J.: Bowker, 1995.

How to choose and read books aloud, share literature through booktalking, creative dramatics, storytelling, and other celebrations, complete with impressive annotated lists of titles, thoroughly indexed by subject.

Kobrin, Beverly. *Eyeopeners! How to Choose and Use Children's Books about Real People, Places, and Things.* New York: Viking, 1988.

Presents more than 500 books that offer factual material in imaginative, enriching, and exciting ways, along with suggestions on how to use them to encourage reading and to enhance a child's innate need to know.

————. *Eyeopeners II: Children's Books to Answer Children's Questions about the World Around Them.* New York: Scholastic, 1995.

This second volume includes nearly 800 newer titles.

Pellowski, Anne. *The Family Storytelling Handbook: How to Use Stories, Anecdotes, Rhymes, Handkerchiefs, Paper, and Other Objects to Enrich Your Family Traditions.* New York: Macmillan, 1987.

A noted collector of multicultural tales offers advice on how and when to tell various types of stories along with a number of examples using papercutting, folded handkerchief, origami, nesting dolls, and fingers.

Reed, Arthea J. S. *Comics to Classics: A Guide to Books for Teens and Preteens,* Updated and rev. ed. New York: Penguin Books, 1994.

An annotated bibliography of fiction and nonfiction titles with tips on how to get teens and preteens excited about reading books.

Thomas, Rebecca L. *Connecting Cultures: A Guide to Multicultural Literature for Children.* New Providence, N.J.: Bowker, 1996.

A helpful annotated bibliography of over sixteen hundred titles (fiction, folktales, poetry, and songs) for children from preschool through twelve years of age—each with a theme, setting, or character from a specific culture outside the United States. Indexed by title, author, illustrator, culture, and age level.

————. *Primaryplots: A Book Talk Guide for Use with Readers Ages 4–8.* New York: Bowker, 1989.

————. *Primaryplots 2: A Book Talk Guide for Use with Readers Ages 4–8.* New Providence, N.J.: Bowker, 1993.

These bibliographic resource guides group related books on a variety of topics by their subject content, offering ideas of ways they can be used to expand children's learning and literary experiences.

Trelease, Jim. *The Read-Aloud Handbook,* 4th ed. New York: Penguin, 1995.

Using real-life anecdotes and research figures, Trelease explains the importance of reading aloud to children from birth through the teenage years, including dos and don'ts that will make the most of your reading experiences. An extensive annotated list of read-alouds is included.

Making Mathematics Fun

Adler, David A. *Fraction Fun.* New York: Holiday House, 1996.

Bright, colorful graphics and simple activities provide a basic introduction to fractions.

Allison, Linda, and Martha Weston. *Eenie Meenie Miney Math.* Boston: Little, Brown, 1993.

A variety of games and hands-on activities that make learning basic mathematical concepts fun. Included are sorting, matching, shapes, counting, pattern recognition, measuring, and more.

Anno, Mitsumasa. *Anno's Math Games; Anno's Math Games II; Anno's Math Games III.* New York: Philomel, 1987, 1989, 1991.

These books use various objects and approaches—string figures, paper folding, puzzles, mazes, etc.—creatively to teach or reinforce math concepts, Look for other shorter books by this author that offer mind-stretching exercises in deduction, permutations, and counting.

Burns, Marilyn. *The I Hate Mathematics! Book.* Boston: Little, Brown, 1982.

Magic tricks, games, riddles, and more to convince kids they love math.

Burns, Marilyn. *Math for Smarty Pants.* Boston: Little, Brown, 1982.

Features games and puzzles to illustrate the fact that there are many ways to be smart when it comes to mathematics.

Daniel, Becky. *Hooray for the Big Book of Math Facts!* Carthage, Ill.: Good Apple, 1990.

Includes a multiplication wheel, diagnostic tests, and answer key, and patterns for unique addition, subtraction, multiplication, and division math facts wheels. Other books in this series

(same publication date) cover: addition, subtraction, multiplication, division, and fractions.

Kaye, Peggy. *Games for Math: Playful Ways to Help Your Child
Learn Math from Kindergarten to Third Grade.* New York: Pan-
theon, 1987.

A collection of games that the teacher/author has played and
used with her students, one-on-one, to help them gain a better
understanding of basic math concepts.

Sharp, Richard M., and Seymour Metzner. *The Sneaky Square and
Other Math Activities,* expanded 2nd ed. New York: TAB Books
(McGraw-Hill), 1996.

This collection of clever math puzzles, problems, and activities
is "designed to arouse children's interest in mathematical activities, provide practice in basic number operations, and encourage creative approaches to solving problems."

Smoothey, Marion. *Let's Investigate Quadrilaterals.* New York: Mar-
shall Cavendish, 1993.

This appealing approach to mathematics features clear, colorful graphic illustrations, games, and activities that make learning the basic concepts fun. Other books in the series are: *Circles;
Numbers; Number Patterns; Area and Volume;* and *Triangles.*

Stienecker, David L. Discovering Math Series. *(Addition; Division;
Fractions; Multiplication; Numbers; Subtraction).* New York:
Benchmark Books, 1996.

Enrichment activities and games designed to help reinforce basic math concepts in an exciting way.

The World Around Us

America the Beautiful series. Chicago: Children's Press, 1987–94.

Each volume of this colorfully illustrated series covers a single
state, featuring information on geography, history, economy,
government, industry, famous people, etc. (Various authors)

Bell, Neil. *Book of Where or How to Be Naturally Geographic.* Boston: Little, Brown, 1982.

Basic concepts of geography such as maps, continental plates,
longitude, and latitude are presented along with humorous

illustrations, interesting text, and entertaining puzzles and games.

Caney, Steven. *Steven Caney's Kids' America*. Workman Publishing, 1978.

Suggests handicraft projects, genealogy searches, and games to introduce aspects of American life from Colonial times to the 1970s.

Celebrate the States series. New York: Benchmark Books, 1997– .

Each volume in this attractive and informative series, created for children nine and older, surveys the geography, history, people, and customs of one state. (Various authors)

Enchantment of the World series. Chicago: Children's Press, various dates.

A well-organized series, with individual volumes on most countries of the world. Many color photos highlight plentiful information that covers history, people, religions, geography, food, special holidays and celebrations, famous people, sports, and other topics, making these books great sources for country reports. (various authors)

Kenda, Margaret, and Phyllis S. Williams. *Geography Wizardry for Kids*. Hauppauge, New York: Barron's Educational Series, 1997.

A wealth of creative, clearly explained, fun-to-do activities designed to help young people understand mapping, exploration, weather, oceans, animals, and people around the world, and more.

Weitzman, David. *My Backyard History Book*. Boston: Little, Brown, 1975.

Digging into the past with stories, games, and activities leads children to explore their family and local history.

Hands-on Science

Allison, Linda, and David Katz. *Gee Wiz! How to Mix Art and Science, or the Art of Thinking Scientifically*. Boston: Little, Brown, 1983.

Through projects using material commonly found around the house, shows how imagination is a vital ingredient in scientific exploration.

Burnie, David. *How Nature Works: 100 Ways Parents and Kids Can Share the Secrets of Nature.* Pleasantville, N.Y.: Reader's Digest, 1991.

> Interesting and exciting adult/child projects and an abundance of information that will make the study of biology a joyful experience. Excellent color photos and drawings and clear diagrams help to introduce basic concepts and experiments.

Hann, Judith. *How Science Works.* Pleasantville, N.Y.: Reader's Digest, 1991.

> Science activities, projects, and information presented in a manner that makes learning fun.

Hauser, Jill Frankel. *Super Science Concoctions: 50 Mysterious Mixtures for Fabulous Fun.* Charlotte, Vt.: Williamson Publishing, 1997.

> More than 75 safe, inexpensive science experiments that illustrate changes in form and chemical composition.

Rockwell, Robert E., Elizabeth A. Sherwood, and Robert Williams. *Hug a Tree and Other Things to Do Outdoors with Young Children.* Mt. Ranier, Md.: Gryphon House, 1983.

> Presents activities that can be used to supplement the environmental education of children.

Scagell, Robin. *Space Explained: A Beginner's Guide to the Universe.* New York: Henry Holt, 1996.

> A basic overview of our solar system—the moon, planets, stars, Milky Way, and other galaxies—including lots of colorful diagrams, paintings, and photos along with numerous informational tidbits.

See How They Grow series. New York: Sony Kids' Video, 1993.

> These outstanding videorecordings, for the preschool/primary audience, bring to life the books of the same series (Dorling Kindersley, 1991–93)—each one focusing on the growth and development of a specific animal. Insects and animals of farm, desert, jungle, sea, and tree are currently available.

Simon, Seymour. *The Brain: Our Nervous System.* New York: Morrow, 1997.

The first of a continuing series on the human body. Large print, exceptional color photos, and clearly written, informative text make this a good general introduction to the subject for children aged six and older. Another title in the series is *The Heart: Our Circulatory System*.

————. *Lightning*. New York: Morrow, 1997.

One title in a continuing series of books on natural disasters that offer a general background along with outstanding full-page color photographs. Other titles are: *Storms; Earthquakes; Volcanoes; Wildfires*.

————. *Mercury*. New York: Morrow, 1992.

One of a series of informative general introductions to the planets and the solar system. Amazing color photographs and large type make this series appealing to all ages.

Sportworks: More Than 50 Fun Games and Activities That Explore the Science of Sports. Reading, Mass.: Addison-Wesley, 1989.

From the Ontario Science Centre in Toronto comes this collection of activities that helps children to examine sports feats and equipment in a scientific manner.

Taylor, Barbara. *Earth Explained: A Beginner's Guide to Our Planet*. New York: Henry Holt, 1997.

A general overview of the Earth, its structure, geological make-up, weather and climate arranged by two-page subtopics (e.g., volcanoes, the world's winds) that include brief information along with excellent cutaway diagrams, clearly labeled drawings, and fascinating facts.

Whitfield, Philip, and Joyce Pope. *Why Did the Dinosaurs Disappear? Questions about Life in the Past Answered by Philip Whitfield with the Natural History Museum*. New York: Viking, 1991.

One of a series of six titles in question-and-answer format from the British Natural History Museum, this volume provides brief answers to many of the questions children ask about dinosaurs and prehistoric life. The other books focus on human anatomy, nature's rhythms and cycles, animals, ecology, and planet Earth.

Notable Series and Books of General Interest

Brown Paper School series. Boston: Little, Brown.

A wide variety of topics, including math, genealogy, the human body, and more. Each volume is packed with tidbits of information and accompanying activities that will keep a good reader fascinated for hours on end.

Brown Paper Preschool series, by Linda Allison. Boston: Little, Brown, 1993–96.

Interactive learning games and activities for parents and their young children. Titles include: *Eeny Meeny Miney Math; Pint-Size Science; Razzle Dazzle Doodle Art; Wordsaroni; Howdy Do Me and You.*

Eye Openers series. New York: Aladdin Books, 1991– .

Appealing color photos and large print highlight these simple introductions to a variety of topics appropriate for preschoolers and beginning readers. Topics include farm animals, diggers and dump trucks, zoo, etc.

Eyewitness Books. Knopf and Dorling Kindersley, 1988– .

A series of large-sized, well-designed books on a myriad of topics that give a good overview of the subject, featuring excellent color photographs with captions that provide as much information as does the brief text. Topics covered range from music, plants, arms and armor, money, and sports, to flags, ancient civilizations, pirates, and various animals. Appropriate for all ages.

Gralla, Preston. *Online Kids: A Young Surfer's Guide to Cyberspace.* New York: John Wiley & Sons, 1996.

Includes a background on the World Wide Web and how to use related services, netiquette and online safety, and lots of annotated sites for homework help and entertainment.

Haslam, Andrew, ed. *Make It Work!* New York: Thomson Learning, 1995– .

Individual volumes on a variety of science, history, and geography topics, such as sound, electricity, machines, photography, time, flight, dinosaurs, ancient Egypt, Arctic peoples.

Attractive, well-designed formats include clear directions for exciting projects that are designed to help children gain an understanding of the topic. Color photos show project materials and the finished product—many including a child doing part of the activity.

Kids Can series. Williamson Publishing, 1989– .

A continuing series of books for parents and teachers to use with children of various ages that offer exciting hands-on learning experiences. Subjects covered include science, gardening, wildlife, cooking, geography, and various topical arts and crafts projects.

Miller, Elizabeth B. *The Internet Resource Directory for K–12 Teachers and Librarians, 95/96 Edition*. Englewood, Colo.: Libraries Unlimited, 1996.

An annotated list of free, regularly updated Web sites organized by subject and intended for use in curriculum enrichment and for professional growth by adults who work with students of various ages. Web sites range from the Alaskan Iditarod Home Page to Civil War Letters to Volcano World.

Reader's Digest. *How in the World*. Pleasantville, N.Y.: Reader's Digest, 1990.

A fascinating journey through the world of human ingenuity.

VanCleave, Janice. Science for Every Kid series. New York: Wiley.

VanCleave, a former science teacher, is a master at introducing the principles of science and mathematics through a variety of activities that hold high appeal for children of various ages. This series—one of several that she has authored—includes volumes on astronomy, biology, chemistry, dinosaurs, earth science, geography, math, and physics.

Web Sites

The only constant thing about the Internet is that it continually changes. Web sites, like libraries, must continue to add new resources in order to stay current and maintain their quality, and exciting new sites will continue to appear as others vanish from the Net. Despite these fluctuations, this *Guide to Homeschooling Resources* would be incomplete without a list of appropriate Web sites. Included here are a few sites for homeschoolers, for parents, and for children that represent the very best of the multitude of sites I have visited while preparing this guide. I offer them as a groundwork that can link you to a world of information, entertainment, adventure, fun, and learning.

For Homeschoolers

Catholic Homeschoolers of Texas
http://www.geocities.com/Athens/Delphi/5329/Index2.html

> Formerly Catholic Home Education Resources, this site includes lists of suppliers of Catholic curriculum, information on national and state Catholic support groups, links to Catholic publishers, homeschooling organizations, supplies, etc.; also family pages of Catholic homeschoolers and other homeschooling Web sites.

The Children's Home Page
http://www.comlab.ox.ac.uk/oucl/users/jonathan.bowen/children.html

> The Bowen family's home page includes the personal pages of the two Bowen girls plus an impressive array of links to museum pages, movie clips for kids, games on the Web, educational and literature sites and home pages of other families (including the "White House for Kids").

Home Education Press
http://www.home-ed-press.com

> Articles from Home Education Magazine, homeschooling information and resources, lists of organizations, support groups, and publishers, state laws, homeschool Web sites, timely news and more.

Homeschool World
http://www.home-school.com/

> From the publishers of *Practical Homeschooling, Homeschool PC,* and *Big Happy Family.* Includes articles about homeschooling, state laws and compliance information, a calendar of homeschool events, homeschool support groups by state or country, a "Homeschool Mall," kids' page, and much more.

The Homeschooling Zone
http://www.caro.net/~joesspa/zonetour.htm

> This guided tour of the zone leads to resources for moms, a marketplace, entertainment, home education help, resources for special needs kids, small business support, and links to some great hand-picked educational sites and "Joe's Cool Web Picks."

Jewish Home Educator's Network
http://snj.com/jhen

> This is the only site that contains information for Jewish home-schoolers. Included are FAQs and information on the Jewish Home Educator's Newsletter.

Jon's Homeschool Resource Page
http://www.midnightbeach.com/hs/

> FAQs, online discussion and support groups, homeschoolers' home pages, national homeschooling organizations and local support groups, and connections to many of the best sites on the net.

Kids at Home
http://www.transport.com/~kidshome/

> This online magazine is a forum for home-schooled children aged four through thirteen, for sharing their writing and art. Each issue also features a published children's author or illustrator and special activities, such as contests and interactive opportunities.

For Parents

Kidsource On-line
http://www.kidsource.com/kidsource/pages/about.html

> Created by "a group of parents who want to make a positive and lasting difference in the lives of parents and children," this site focuses primarily on health- and education-related issues. Sections relating to newborns through high school aged children, education and health, recreation, parenting, software, and more offer a wealth of information. Visitors to this site can participate in forums on education, software, and more. Of special note is "The Super Sitter," a detailed guide for babysitters.

**The Librarian's Guide to Cyberspace for Parents and Kids/50+
Great Sites for Kids and Parents**
http://www.ssdesign.com/parentspage/greatsites/50.html

> The American Library Association offers this array of sites recommended by librarians for preschool through elementary aged children and their parents.

Log on @ the Library
http://www.ssdesign.com/ALAKids/lol.shtml#childsafe

> The American Library Association offers advice for parents regarding their children's introduction to and safe use of the Internet.

National Parent Information Network
http://ericps.ed.uiuc.edu/npin/npinhome.html

> The purpose of this site, which is sponsored by the ERIC Clearinghouse on Elementary and Early Childhood Education and the Clearinghouse on Urban Education, is "to provide information to parents and those who work with parents and to foster the exchange of parenting materials." Included are full text of articles, reviews and abstracts of books and hyperlinks to periodicals on parenting, as well as Internet resources, a parenting discussion list, "Parents AskERIC" question answering service, and much more.

The Parents' Guide to the Information Superhighway
http://www.childrenspartnership.org/parentsguide/partI.html

> This site, sponsored by the Children's Partnership, offers a thorough introduction to computers and the Internet and tips on how to introduce computers and guide their use by children from age two through eighteen. Also included are rules for safe use of the Internet and netiquette.

For Children

Children's Literature Web Guide
http://www.ucalgary.ca/~dkbrown/index.html

> Lots of links to literature-related sites, including home pages of children's authors and illustrators with e-mail connections.

The Education Connection

http://peabody.vanderbilt.edu/projects/proposed/asd/ecnew/page5.htm

This exciting educational Web site offers links to "Great Web Sites" for students and educators on topics such as visual and performing arts (piano on the Net, discovery of a Paleolithic painted cave); college and career opportunities; virtual tours; and "Challenge Zones" that present science information. In addition, links to the nation's K–12 schools, associations serving children, educators, departments of education in all fifty states, and tools for teachers, parents, and students (e.g., homework assignment sheets and certificates to download).

Kids Web

http://www.npac.syr.edu/textbook/kidsweb

The Kids Web goal is to present students with a subset of the Web that is very simple to navigate and contains information targeted at the K–12 level. Topics are: the arts, the sciences, games, reference, sports, social studies, and miscellaneous. There are also links to external lists of material on each subject that more advanced students can browse for further information.

School Topics

http://www.asd.k12.ak.us/Homepages/JAndrews/TeacherTopics.html

School Topics offers a list of teaching units on various subjects, with many links to sites relating to each topic. Useful to parents as well as children, it provides a multitude of ideas for educational instruction and enrichment.

Susan G. Scheps, a supervisor of children's services at the Shaker Heights (Ohio) Public Library, is editor of *Homeschoolers and the Public Library: A Resource Guide for Libraries Serving Homeschoolers* (PLA, 1993). As cochair of the Parent Education Services Committee (Adult Lifelong Learning Section, 1991–93) she was responsible for organizing the second of two programs on public library/home-schooler relations presented by that committee at the ALA Conference in New Orleans in 1993. She has written and edited a column for the *Journal of Youth Services in Libraries* and reviewed books for *School Library Journal* for the past fourteen years.